Expert Witness Handbook

Expert Witness Handbook

Tips and Techniques for the Litigation Consultant

Dan Poynter

- Advice

- Explanations

- Guidelines

- Checklists

- Examples

- Resources

 Para Publishing, Santa Barbara, California

Expert Witness Handbook

Tips and Techniques for the Litigation Consultant

by Dan Poynter

Published by

Para Publishing
Post Office Box 4232
Santa Barbara, CA 93140-4232 USA
Telephone: (805) 968-7277

Library of Congress Cataloging-in-Publication Data
Poynter, Dan.
    Expert Witness Handbook

    Bibliography: p.
    Includes index.
    1. Evidence, Expert--United States. I. Title.
KF8961.P69 1987 347.73'67 87-2279
ISBN 0-915516-45-4 Hardcover 347.30767

Table of Contents

About the Author

Dan Poynter is an expert witness. He has served as a technical expert in the field of parachutes and skydiving since 1973. Though this is a narrow area of expertise, he has counselled on scores of cases and has testified many times. This book is full of the inside nut-and-bolts tips only a *participant* could know.

Since 1962, Dan Poynter has also been a *participant* in the parachute field. With 1,200 jumps and every license, rating and award, he has written six books on the subject. Two parachute books have been translated into other languages. Politically active in the sport, he has served on virtually every committee and has been elected Chairman of the Board of the U.S. Parachute Association and President of the Parachute Industry Association. His credibility as an expert witness is verified by his experience in the sport and leadership in the industry.

Dan Poynter has a BA and two years of post-graduate work in law. The author of more than 400 magazine articles and 27 books, he is an author and publisher first and a technical expert second. His work as an author over the last 25 years has allowed him to study his subjects in detail while validating his expertise. He lives in Santa Barbara, California, and works throughout North America.

The author was prompted to write this book because so many people approached him for information on litigation consulting.

Introduction

Whether you are a seasoned veteran or a newcomer to the expert witness business, you will use this book again and again. It tells you how to get started, how to decide whether or not to accept a case, how to conduct yourself at a deposition or in court, what to charge, how to collect payments, and much more.

Of course, experience is the best teacher. Your own expertise will grow with every case you work on. But this book will help you get started. To increase your knowledge and effectiveness, you will also want to attend expert witness conferences, talk to other experts, and keep on reading. (You will find a suggested book list in the resource section of the Appendix of this book.)

Because laws differ from jurisdiction to jurisdiction and every case is unique, I offer the following caveats:

Different attorneys handle cases in different ways. It is up to them to deal with the differences and exceptions. Always clear *good ideas* with your client-attorney before proceeding.

Each state and the federal courts have differing rules on whether experts have to be named, whether experts can be deposed by the other side, if acceptance of the risk, signing of a waiver or contributory negligence is a valid defense, etc. Some specialties, such as medicine, have exceptional rules. This book cannot possibly list all of the differences and exceptions but it does provide the best general interpretation of most topics of interest to the expert.

Throughout this text, examples of lawyer-witness exchanges are presented for illustrative purposes. Several peer reviewers of the manuscript commented that these questions and answers were one of the most interesting and valuable parts of the book. These exchanges are not necessarily correct, proper or suggested by the author as answers to the questions. Since every case, court setting and opposing attorney are different, some replies may be appropriate while others are not. They are offered here to educate, stimulate and provoke thought. All have been used by experts — with varying degrees of success.

If you have any questions concerning any of the statements in this book, your client-attorney or other qualified professional is the best source for a complete answer.

Welcome to the challenge of litigation consulting.

Dan Poynter
Santa Barbara

Foreword

This important book will serve as a valuable introduction for the neophyte expert witness as well as resource for the seasoned litigation consultant.

Most books devoted to this subject have been written for the attorney whose use of the litigation consultant and expert witness grows more and more each year. Here now is a book specifically written for the expert witness by an experienced expert!

Whether you decide to pursue expert witness work, or are simply invited to serve as an expert at some time in your career, this book will help you to evaluate your own potential as well as to perform the job professionally and successfully.

I strongly believe that litigation consultants should put something back into the system through teaching, writing, consulting or other industry participation. Dan is doing just that with this book.

I know this book will stimulate the orderly growth of the litigation consulting field. It is long overdue.

Betty S. Lipscher
National Forensic Center
Lawrenceville, New Jersey

Acknowledgment

I would like to thank the following for their contributions to this book:

My peer reviewers: document analysis expert M. Patricia Fisher, bicycle expert John Forester, aircraft accident reconstruction and analysis expert Ira Rimson, media analysis expert Marilyn A. Lashner, Ph.D., land use expert Eugene D. Wheeler, AICP, litigation (patent) attorney Harvey Jacobson, Jr., litigation (family law) attorney Sterling E. Myers, litigation (aviation) attorney J. Scott Hamilton, litigation (personal injury) attorney Joseph T. Mallon, and Professor Oliver C. Schroeder, Jr. of Case Western Reserve University.

My three able assistants, Judy Egenolf, Pat Finn and Monique Tihanyi who make Para Publishing run and give me time to write.

To Microsoft *Word* and my Compaq 286 for speeding my writing and checking my spelling, Sandy Stryker for the heavy manuscript rewrite, *RightWriter* and Pat Finn for copy editing, Xerox *Ventura Publisher* for typesetting, and Mindy Bingham, publisher of Advocacy Press, for ideas and support.

To Betty Lipscher and the National Forensic Center for hosting the annual Expert Witness Conferences. Her Conference introduced me to dynamic people, bolstered my enthusiasm for litigation consulting and gave me the idea for this book.

I sincerely thank all these fine people and I know they are proud of the part they have played in litigation consulting as well as in the development of this book.

Warning

This book is designed to provide information in regard to the subject matter covered. It is sold with the understanding that the publisher and author are not engaged in rendering legal, accounting or other professional services. If legal or other expert assistance is required, the services of a competent professional should be sought.

It is not the purpose of this manual to reprint all the information that is otherwise available to the expert witness but to complement, amplify and supplement other texts. For more information, see the many references in the Appendix.

Every effort has been made to make this manual as complete and as accurate as possible. However, there **may be mistakes** both typographical and in content. Therefore, this text should be used only as a general guide and not as the ultimate source on the subject. Furthermore, this manual contains information on the subject only up to the printing date.

The purpose of this manual is to educate and entertain. The author and Para Publishing shall have neither liability nor responsibility to any person or entity with respect to any loss or damage caused or alleged to be caused directly or indirectly by the information contained in this book. When in doubt, ask your client-attorney.

Laws and philosophies will change. The author cannot predict what legislatures and courts will decide after this book is printed.

If you do not agree with the above, you may return this book to the publisher for a full refund.

Disclaimer

CHAPTER ONE

What is an Expert Witness and Why be One?

If something can break, bend, crack, fold, spindle, mutilate, smolder, disintegrate, radiate, malfunction, embarrass, besmirch, infect or explode, there is someone, somewhere who can explain how and why. These people are often asked to take part in legal actions. There are litigation consultants on jogging, bicycles, dancing, solid waste management, speaking, writing, human bites, coastal planning and even skydiving. These experts investigate and explain to the attorney and later they explain or *teach* the subject to the judge and jury.

In court cases, a gemologist may be called in to evaluate jewelry, a toxicologist may explain the effects of alcohol in a drunk driving case, or a retired police officer may describe the sequence of events in a traffic accident.

There are two kinds of witnesses: lay witnesses and expert witnesses. Lay *eyewitnesses* to the event may only tell what they saw, heard, felt or smelled; they are not allowed to tell what others have said or say what they think of the case. An expert *technical* witness, on the other hand, is allowed to express opinion on any relevant issue falling within the scope of his or her expertise. The expert witness need not have been there when it happened. The expert is presumed to be an impartial, disinterested person who is simply explaining why and how things happen.

Why would anyone want to be an expert witness? Five reasons come to mind:

1. To capitalize on your years of education and experience. Serving as a litigation consultant is a way to do more work in the field you enjoy; another way to make money on what you already know by *pyramiding* your expertise. It enables you to develop a lucrative sideline that could lead to a post-retirement career. Perhaps you are already a consultant and are searching for another profit center. Litigation consulting has been called *a prestigious way to moonlight.*

2. To experience the challenge, drama and excitement of dealing with people's lives, large sums of money or even the the course of history.

3. To put something back into the system. That is, to help people in your field.

4. To get paid for further study. Since you must anticipate every deposition and trial question, you will have to conduct research, study and write. This bank of material may later be used in articles and books. You are being paid for this study time so it is all quite nice if you love your subject.

5. To make money. Expert witness work pays well. It may take up 10% of your time but contribute 20% or more of your income, and there is no investment in inventory .

Perhaps none of these reasons apply to you. Maybe you work for one of the parties to the suit and are being called to testify about company procedures. This could be the only deposition or trial you attend. If so, you may wish to jump ahead to Chapter Four.

An expert witness or litigation consultant is someone skilled in a particular art, trade or profession or with special information or expertise in a particular subject area. The expert assists the client-attorney in understanding and presenting the technical aspects of the case.

The impact of a technical expert in trial proceedings is three-fold:

1. The expert explains the logic of the mechanism involved, be it a technique, mechanical or medical procedure

2. The expert gives an authoritative opinion as to causation and fault, if any

3. The expert, by his or her mere presence, enlarges the importance of the case.

Attorneys and courts are relying on expert witnesses more and more to help them understand complex matters or little known procedures. It is far less expensive for an attorney to call in an expert for a custom-tailored short-course in the subject than to spend months or years trying to learn a new field. The attorney has to know enough about the subject to effectively cross-examine the opposing lay and expert witnesses.

Expert witnesses are put on the stand not only for what they conclude based on the facts in the case, but for what they know about general practices that shed light on the matter at hand.

You may be retained before trial to assist counsel in investigating and understanding the facts. Since some 97% of your cases will be settled out of court, your primary work will be as a consultant. After you investigate the case and make a report to the client-attorney, the attorney may alter the case strategy. You will go to court only when neither side has a clear edge.

The expert may also be retained by that attorney or the court to educate the jury. The expert will help the jury understand the technical aspects of the case and will try to persuade the jury to accept his or her explanation of the technical facts.

Experts are often used in out-of-court dispute resolutions, as well. Two-thirds of the experts recently polled by the National Forensic Center have performed out-of-court work.

And just as the state must provide an attorney to the indigent in criminal cases, now those who cannot afford to pay have a right to a state-paid expert to support their criminal case. There is a lot of work out there for expert witnesses and the demand is expected to grow.

Many experts are independent consultants. Others work for large *forensic engineering* firms which provide a wide range of services.

Being an expert witness for the first time can be an interesting but frightening experience. You may have heard of colleagues who have experienced brilliant victories or humbling defeats in court. If done properly, the job can be personally satisfying and rewarding.

Basically, expert witnesses provide four types of services:

1. They **investigate** the particular scene or event, research everything written on the subject, run tests and then analyze and evaluate their findings.

2. They **evaluate** the merits of a potential claim and document their work with a written report on their findings. They express their opinion about the cause of the problem and merits of the claim.

3. They **recommend** certain aspects of litigation strategy. The client-attorney may not be suing the right party. The expert may know more about the law in this specific area because experts tend to collect articles and citations on matters of interest to them. They will suggest other areas to be investigated or tested. They probably know the opposing expert and can project the arguments that he or she may use. These recommendations make the expert a valuable assistant to the client-attorney.

4. They **testify** in depositions and at trial to explain and then defend the technical conclusions they have reached. The Federal Trade Commission even allows expert witnesses to cross-examine opposing witnesses before an administrative law judge. This is presumably because they know their subjects better than the lawyers.

Since about 97% of the cases never go to trial, most of the expert witnesses' time is spent in investigation and evaluation.

Experts explain to the client-attorney (and later to the judge and jury)

- scientific and technical issues

- issues concerning *practice in the trade*

- the meaning of certain terminology under *trade usage*

- damages issues — estimating lost value or profits caused by the defendant's wrongful conduct.

Do you have what it takes? To be an expert witness, you must have a field of expertise (see Chapter Two) and you must be:

- Inquisitive. Be the type of person who wants to know why things happen. You must enjoy doing library research and running tests. You must have access to reliable sources of information and be able to absorb and evaluate what you learn.

- A writer. You must be able to put your thoughts on paper; to express yourself well. Since you are selling information, your most important tool is your word processor.

- A good speaker. Be able to think on your feet so that you can express your opinion and respond quickly to defend your position. You must be articulate and able to think clearly under the pressure of cross-examination. After continued badgering by an opposing attorney, one expert replied as follows:

Opposing attorney: *You haven't told us everything today, have you?*
Expert: *No sir, I haven't told you everything. It would be impossible to condense 25 years of experience into three hours of testimony.*

- A teacher. You need to show counsel, the opposing side, judge and jury why your findings are correct. You should be a good performer; you must be able to persuade.

You must be creative enough to provide new perspectives on the case to your client-attorney.

• Mediagenic. There is a difference between honesty and believability. Just knowing your subject and being truthful are not enough. You must be able to win over your audience. Certainly Ronald Reagan has taught us how important being mediagenic is to selling a program.

• Able to reason. Experts have to be able to deduce correct inferences from hypothetically stated facts or from facts involving scientific or technical knowledge.

• Credibility. Credibility comes from expertise in the specific subject required, qualifications such as a degree or title, integrity, knowledge, and speaking/teaching ability.

Bicycle expert John Forester frequently refers to a quotation from Francis Bacon that hangs over his desk:

Reading maketh a full man,
conference a ready man, and
writing an exact man.

Being a litigation consultant requires all of these.

Who can be an expert? Expert witness work is not for everyone. Some people rise to the challenge while many find the experience distressing.

Practicing lawyers tend to make bad witnesses, lay or expert. They can be condescending, uncooperative in case preparation and perceived as untrustworthy. Legal training develops rational patterns of thought rather than scientific ones. This is why legal professionals rarely hire other lawyers to testify as experts. On the other hand, technical experts with law degrees who are not practicing lawyers can be very good witnesses.

To qualify as an expert witness, you must have something unique to contribute. Your qualifications may be academic or operational, local or national, general or specific.

Many people have an expertise in some field. Almost any skill or discipline will qualify; you do not need a professional or academic degree. Naturally, some skills and disciplines are in greater demand than others. You may be an expert because of your background, experience or knowledge. Since most cases will involve difficult questions, you should be exceptionally competent in whatever field you offer your services. Attorneys, judges and juries will evaluate your ability by your public qualifications. More specifically they will consider your:

• Education, training or practical experience (have you done it?)

• Professional and technical expertise

• Job position and function

• Recognition by other bodies such as professional associations. What awards have you received?

• Publications: books or articles (you have committed your knowledge to paper to teach others). The public seems to perceive anyone who has written a book as an expert

• Licenses or registrations held. If there are certifications in your field of expertise, you must secure them. Many courts will not admit testimony from unlicensed people.

Even if admitted, juries will not give such testimony much weight

- Memberships in professional societies

- Accomplishments

- Research in the field

or any combination of the above.

Many expert witnesses find their work to be very rewarding. The challenges are considerable, the technical problems are complex and the money is good. Enlarging your practice to include litigation consulting may be the best career decision you could make.

For clarity, the *trier of fact* will be referred to as *the jury* throughout this text. In non-jury *court trials*, the judge is both the trier of fact as well as the trier of law. See the Glossary.

**A collage of three columns of 226 from
the Forensic Services Directory**

CHAPTER TWO

How to Get Started

To get started, you need to do two things: identify your subject area and let the lawyers know you are available.

Selecting a field. Your area of expertise should be obvious to you. Chances are it has to do with your work or the hobbies you pursue. Attorneys seek experts in the following areas:

• Experts on specific areas of activity: for example, skydiving training, bicycle design or equine nutrition

• Experts on the mechanics of injury

• Experts in human factors who understand the plaintiff's inability to recognize a hazard, evaluate the unreasonableness of a risk, or the economy or value (technical or social) of an engineering alternative

• Accident reconstruction experts

• Test experts

- Medical experts

- Economic loss and evaluation experts

- Experts in rehabilitation problems and potentialities

- Researchers for literature searches

- Experts on a standard of care in a particular industry or area of knowledge.

Many people know a great deal about something. Use your expertise but do not venture beyond it. Limit your practice to those specific areas in which you are outstanding and where you plan to continue your education. For example, choose helicopters, not aviation. Better yet, choose rotor hubs, if this is your specialty. You cannot be an expert on piloting, navigation, propellers, airframes, and engines, both jet and reciprocating. The narrower your field, the more believable you will be and the less competition you will have. See the *Forensic Services Directory* published by the National Forensic Center for a list of specialties.

Marketing yourself. Once you decide to be an expert witness, you must let the legal world know of your availability. Spread word of your interest wherever attorneys are likely to look: in expert directories, at universities, in professional and technical societies, at other firms in the industry, private consulting firms or other lawyers.

To advertise your availability do some or all of the following:

1. **Directory Listings.** Send your curriculum vita (resume), fee schedule and some promotional literature on your regular line of work to each of the directories and registries

listed in the Appendix of this book. See Chapter Fifteen on drafting a curriculum vita and Chapter Twelve on fee schedules.

Once you receive applications from these directories, visit your local *law* library; it is probably in the county courthouse. If the county seat is a long way off, a university law school may be more accessible. Ask to see the expert witness directories. Review the areas of expertise listed and photocopy the pages that interest you. Use the photocopies to determine the best place to be listed and to draft a competitive listing.

Some of the registries listed in the Appendix are *expert brokerages*. For example, Technical Advisory Service for Attorneys (TASA) maintains a list of some 6,000 experts in more than 1,600 specialties. Once they accept you, they pass your name on to lawyers needing assistance. You work through TASA and they mark-up your usual rate.

In contrast, the *Forensic Services Directory*, published by the National Forensic Center, is a place to list your availability and qualifications. Interested attorneys contact you and contract with you directly. Some directory listings are free while some publishers charge a fee.

Fish, Frederick, A.
33 Tributary Road
Big Creek, WY 82999
(307) 555-1212
Specialties: Drowning accident reconstruction; Report & deposition interpretation; Data on the sensations of drowning. **Affiliations:** Aquatic Safety Experts, USCG Cmdr. (ret.). **Degrees & Licenses:** BS, WSI.

Example of a directory listing

Code your address when you draft your directory listings. For example, use P.O. Box 4232-B or 48 Walker Street, Suite 712. Do not use *department*. This coding is too obvious and many people will not use it. With codes you will know what kind of a return you are receiving from each directory and advertisement. Next year you may alter your advertising to reflect your results.

2. **Mailings.** Send your curriculum vita, fee schedule and any promotional literature on your regular line of work with a cover letter to attorneys in your field. For example, if your area of expertise is parachuting, send your packet to aviation lawyers. Do not mail to every lawyer in sight. Use the most specific lists possible.

The American Bar Association rents its mailing list of 500,000 lawyers by areas of specialization. For information, contact the ABA, 750 North Lake Shore Drive, Chicago, IL 60611 (312) 988-5435. Contact all the associations listed in the Appendix for mailing list information.

December 11, 1988

Ladies and Gentlemen:

I am offering my services as an expert witness in mouse trap technology.

The attached material outlines my experience in this field. Please place this information on file for future reference.

Very truly yours,

Michael J. Maus, R.R.

MJM/mm

Letter offering consulting services

3. **Attend meetings** in your area of expertise. Most people find court room work unpleasant. Let your colleagues know you are open to this kind of work. Tell your national associations and magazine editors. Then when lawyers come looking for an expert, you will not only be referred, you will be recommended.

4. **Write articles** in your area of expertise. Let the magazines spread your name around. Lawyers will find you through periodical indexes.

5. **Take a course** in accident investigation. Get to know other experts and lawyers in your field. Lawyers often consult other lawyers first when looking for a particular type of expert. This method makes sense as they can not only find an expert but can ask if he or she is any good. Check local colleges for these courses.

6. **Advertising.** If you are in a wide field, such as accounting, and expect most of your cases to be local, advertise in the *Yellow Pages.* List yourself under *Attorneys' Services* as well as under *Accountants.* If your area is narrower and you expect to work in a wide geographical area, try some of the specialized law journals. See the listings in the Appendix and check the magazines in your local law library. Place your ads where you see ads from other expert witnesses. To obtain sample copies of magazines, send a letter like the following:

December 17, 1988

Trial Magazine
1050 31st Street NW
Washington, DC 20007

Ladies and Gentlemen:

Your publication is being considered as an advertising medium for our services. Please forward a media package to include:

1. Display advertising rate card
2. Classified advertising rate card
3. Current circulation figures (ABC statement)
4. Schedule of special editions
5. Two different sample copies of your publication so that we may determine the best size and placement for our advertising.

Do you provide discounts or special rates for new advertisers?

We would appreciate being placed on file to be notified of any future rate or policy change.

Very truly yours,

Letter for obtaining sample magazines and ad rates

7. **Speaking.** Arrange to be a speaker at a law seminar in your area. Let the attorneys see and hear you as well as learn about your area of expertise.

8. **Write a book.** In looking for an expert, lawyers often check for books written in that area of expertise. They simply look in the Subject Guide of *Books In Print* available at the reference desk of your public library. It lists all the books currently available on any given subject.

Of course, there are other benefits to authoring a book. The prestige enjoyed by the published author is unparalleled in our society. A book can bring recognition, income and an acceleration in one's career. Once you are a published author, many people will consider you to be an expert on that subject.

For more information on book writing, see *Is There a Book Inside You?* by Dan Poynter and Mindy Bingham. For more information on book publishing, see *The Self-Publishing Manual* by Dan Poynter. There is an order blank on the last page of this book.

9. **Referrals.** As your expert witness work increases, more and more of your new business will come from referrals. As you become known, and as word of your work spreads, people will recommend you.

Now, sit back and wait for the calls — but do not rest. Constantly review your promotion to see where improvements can be made.

CHAPTER THREE

Contracting To Work

It is important to establish a system to formalize the business relationship so that you and your client-attorney both understand precisely who hired you, when you are hired and what you are hired for.

There are many things you may be asked to do for the client-attorney besides testifying. You may make literature searches, run tests, build demonstration models for court, advise the client-attorney about the strategy and/or theory of the case, draft questions for interrogatories and depositions and much more. You may simply read some documents and give an opinion or you may do a lot of hand-holding.

Initial contact. The attorney in search of an expert will either call or write you. If he or she knows (from past experience or attorney referral) you have worked on similar cases, you may receive a copy of the complaint and a cover letter asking if you are interested. If he or she is not sure you are qualified, you will probably receive a telephone call.

The attorney will be searching for the best expert. He or she should be looking for someone:

• With expertise in the specific subject area in which an opinion is needed

• Who is competent in that field

• Who has integrity

• With the ability to communicate specialized knowledge to lay people. The jury will probably go with the more credible expert. The attorney wants someone who is *court-wise*

• Who lives nearby, to control travel costs. If your area of expertise is very specific, the calling attorney may have to search a wider area but will still be looking for the best but nearest expert witness.

The calling attorney will try to judge your abilities. If he or she has done some homework on the subject, you may be *cross-examined* like an adversary at trial.

You too may wish to investigate the potential client-attorney and case before you agree to take the case. It is no fun and it certainly won't help your professional reputation to deal with an incompetent attorney or one without integrity. Part of your decision to accept a case will be based on your judgment of the caller's lawyer-like characteristics. Listen carefully to the telephone voice. Does he or she sound polished?

Is this a widely-known, well-established firm? Why is this a one-person firm? Is he or she new in the game? Has he or she been unable to attract other good lawyers? Or is the caller part of a small but aggressive firm with a good reputation? Check with other experts and attorneys. Look up the calling attorney in *Martindale-Hubbel Law Directory*. See the listing in the Appendix. A great part of your decision to accept or reject the case should depend on your judgment about the case and how the calling attorney addresses it. Is the caller trying to push you toward a favorable conclusion? Is the caller unreasonable to work with? If, at any time, you realize the client-attorney is incompetent, unreasonable or dishonest, sever the relationship.

A responsible client-attorney wants to know as soon as possible if the case is weak. He or she is relying on the expert to point out both strengths and weaknesses. The expert is providing a screening service. If the case is weak, the attorney will want to cut losses and save money. Plaintiffs may drop cases or not even file them and defendants may be encouraged to settle. Expert witnesses are not hired to bring good news or to draw out cases, they are hired to provide an objective opinion.

Early calls are essential. Too often, experts receive calls from attorneys a week before the trial. Late calls place an undue burden on the expert. The client-attorney should search for and hire an expert as early in the case as possible for several good reasons:

● The expert can quickly educate the client-attorney with an inexpensive background *short-course* on the general subject. No attorney can be an expert in every subject.

● The expert needs time to conduct investigations and tests to be able to establish reliable opinions and generate accurate reports.

• The expert is a source of information regarding the theories of recovery as well as who could be named as defendants. As part of the industry, the expert is in a better position to know of other past or pending cases with similar issues.

• The expert may assist in the discovery proceedings. He or she may recommend questions for the other expert, anticipate questions and help prepare witnesses for his or her side.

• The expert can assist in answering interrogatories. His or her information could avoid a summary judgment. Analyzing the opposition's discovery requests may reveal their trial theories.

• The expert knows where to find the relevant books, articles, standards and other resource material.

• Having an expert on board may enhance the settlement value of the claim. It is usually less expensive to conclude the case earlier.

• Experts usually take cases on a first-come, first-served basis. Tying up the top specialist early in the case prevents the expert from working on the other side.

Unfortunately, your initial contact with an attorney in search of an expert will often go like this:

The attorney will call, give a few basic details and say: *Based on what you have heard, what do you think?*

Expert: *I will send you my curriculum vita, other materials and fee schedule. If you like what I send, send me a $500 retainer fee and all the paperwork. I will let you know within a few days if I will take the case.* Do not give an opinion. Instead, tell the caller what additional information you need.

Attorney: *Well are you interested in the case?*

Expert: *I can't tell you. Send the information (complaint, interrogatories, depositions, equipment, police report, coroner's report, witness statements, etc.) and the retainer. I will evaluate them, report to you and will tell you if I am interested in the case.* Be firm.

Now, this is the way the call should go:

1. Get full names of plaintiff and defendant, date and place of the incident and the name and firm of the opposing attorney. Make sure you have not been engaged by the other side. Does this attorney represent the plaintiff or defendant?

2. Ask for a brief description of the case. What are the issues? Make sure it is something you can handle. If you cannot, suggest another expert. If you do not like the case, turn it down. Take notes. Ask a few intelligent questions or suggest courses of action to show you know what you are talking about.

When you first talk to the attorney, do not hesitate to reveal your limitations. Make sure he or she understands your background. Do not pretend to be someone you are not. If you are not fully qualified, you will be embarrassed in court.

If you have any conflicts of interest or skeletons in your closet, say so. Do you know any of the parties personally? If you have written articles supporting the calling attorney's position, your stand prior to being contacted will add to your credibility. If you have ever taken a contrary position in testimony or publications, how can you argue the change in your position? Opposing attorneys will research your background and may throw any skeletons back at you.

3. Find out whether you will be working for the attorney or client. Clients may be harder to collect from than attorneys. Incidentally, once you have been hired by an attorney, you may be contacted by other attorneys representing clients on the same side of the action. Always tell your client-attorney and obtain permission to cooperate. Open a separate file for the new client-attorney and make sure he or she will be responsible for the bill.

4. What is the schedule? Has a court date been set? Is your calendar open?

Some experts ask the calling attorney to send only the file for evaluation and ask not to be told which side the calling attorney is on. This approach works especially well in medical cases where there is a file to study. It allows the expert to be more objective.

At this point, you are only agreeing to evaluate the case, you are not agreeing to testify.

You may find that you are not hired in 40% or more of the cases on which you have been contacted. There are several reasons why this is so. You may not be qualified on the precise area of expertise they need, or perhaps your interpretation of the facts does not support the case of the calling attorney.

In contracting, be formal, firm and direct. This will give the attorney more confidence in you and may scare off the irresponsible caller. Your client-attorney wants to deal with a professional who solves problems, not an amateur who creates them.

Send your curriculum vita, fee schedule, brochures on your major line of work and cover letter in a flat 9x12 envelope. Do not fold them. A sample cover letter follows:

February 29, 1989

Hunter and Prey
Daniel J. Hunter, Esquire
1300 North Dos Pueblos
Chumash, CA 93778

<u>Lunch v. Dinner</u>

Dear Mr. Hunter:

Thank you for your letter dated October 14th regarding my availability in the above referenced case.

Enclosed, please find my curriculum vita., brochure on my major line of work and fee schedule.

Please send me a copy of the complaint, interrogatories, depositions, statements, photographs, reports and any other non-confidential information you may have so that I may form an opinion. Also, please send a check for $500. so I may formally open this file.

After reviewing the materials you send, I will call you with my first impressions and will tell you if I will be able to help you in this case.

Very truly yours,

RABBITS UNLIMITED

John Hare, Jr.
Owner

JH/pr

Example of cover letter

Evaluate yourself and the case.

● Are you competent to render an opinion in this particular area?

● Do you need more information?

● What are the weaknesses of the case and can they be diluted or overcome?

● What are the strengths of the case?

● Do you want to run more tests?

● Do you want to prepare some demonstrative evidence?

● Do you need some reference material?

● Can you suggest a reading list to educate the client-attorney?

● Do you have any conflicts of interest?

● Is the calling client-attorney being candid? If you are not receiving all the information or if you have any doubt about the ethical status of the case, you should reject it.

A retainer is an advance payment for future work. It would be more accurate to call this an *advance payment against future billings*, but *retainer* is commonly used in the trade. By requiring an advance payment, you formalize the agreement. People who put up money know they are buying something.

Abraham Lincoln said *A lawyer's time and advice are his stock-in-trade.* Many lawyers display these words in their offices as a reminder to clients. The quote is equally true of the expert witness, and lawyers (as well as their clients) must appreciate that.

Some expert witnesses ask for another advance payment when the first runs out and further require a minimum account maintenance balance. This is often the case when they anticipate extensive charges. They do not want to spend scores of hours on a full case workup and then have collection problems because the case has been settled or otherwise terminated. Or, they may anticipate collection problems because of the type of client or case.

If you have been hired directly by the attorney's client, he or she may not be as familiar with contracting as an attorney. You may spend small amounts of time or expend small amounts of money anticipating rapid reimbursement, but do not extend too much credit. See Chapter Twelve on fees and Chapter Thirteen on collections.

Estimate what it will cost to read depositions and other materials, perform investigations and run tests. Charge by the hour to read case materials. The client-attorney knows the more material he or she sends, the more time you will spend reading. But only the expert knows what special investigations and tests should be conducted to determine and demonstrate the cause of the accident. The amount an attorney is willing to pay for more research and case preparation will depend on the size and importance of the case. Do not spend more time on the case until you reach an agreement on the estimate. See the sample letter, which follows:

February 29, 1988

Lunch v. Dinner

Dear Mr. Lyon:

To properly investigate the above referenced case, I feel we should conduct the following searches and tests. The itemized list below includes estimated time and costs.

1.
2.
3.

We are ready to proceed as soon as we hear from you.

Very truly yours,

Abbreviated sample estimate letter

Tell your client-attorney what tests you want to run and what research you feel you should do. Let the attorney decide if the money should be spent. Cover yourself.

Fees have to be controlled—understood by both sides. With proper communication, the attorney will not have to explain unexpectedly high costs to the client.

Knowledge is power. You want to be the best-informed person in the courtroom; to know more about the case than the attorneys, the judge and even the clients. With more knowledge, you will be comfortable in your role and able to answer any question to the satisfaction of all. Experienced judges and lawyers who are heavyweights in their own fields recognize heavyweights in specialized fields of expertise by the way they carry themselves. You want to project knowledge, confidence and expertise. So do not cut corners or take shortcuts. There is little demand for expert witnesses who make mistakes.

Client-attorney: *This is a simple case so you won't require a great deal of preparation.*

Expert: *I have not earned my reputation by losing cases and I am not about to begin with yours. If you do not intend to prepare properly, I do not want to go into court with you. I will not go into court unprepared.*

Fees. How much you can charge for your knowledge is discussed in detail in Chapter Twelve. The best way to make sure your client-attorney understands your fees and terms is to give him or her a copy of your fee schedule in writing.

Meeting with your client-attorney. The calling attorney will probably offer to drop by or will ask you to visit when next in the area. The attorney wants to size you up before hiring you for deposition or trial testimony. Dress your best and study the case.

Listing witnesses. Some attorneys will bluff the opposing side by saying they have hired you and that you are prepared to testify in support of their case. If you are well-known in the field, just having you on board may cause the other side to cave in.

Some attorneys contact every expert in the field in order to tie them up. They may hire the expert to evaluate a case and render a preliminary opinion. If the opinion is adverse, the attorney may decide to keep the expert as a *consultant* on the case. That way, the expert can't work for the other side. His consulting work for the client-attorney may be considered *attorney work product* since he is not scheduled to testify in court. Attorney work product is confidential (not discoverable) as explained in Chapter Eight on Discovery.

Other attorneys contact several experts, place them on their witness list and then never use them. Or they may list every expert in the field on their witness list without even contacting those witnesses. This keeps the other side very busy looking for a qualified expert.

If an attorney ever involves your name with no intent of hiring you to testify, you may be entitled to damages.

Accepting the case. To agree to work on a case, you may send a letter like the sample below. A written agreement is the safest way to proceed. Often, you simply accept a case during a telephone conversation and the client-attorney sends a letter confirming that you are hired.

February 30, 1988

Lunch v. Dinner

Dear Mr. Lyon:

This letter will confirm your retention of me as an expert to assist your firm in the above referenced case.

We will accept the case based on our published rate (fee schedule dated January 1987) of $140/ hour and $700/day.

We will perform investigation, testing, report writing and testimony at your direction.

After the investigation, we will issue an oral opinion. This report will be followed by a written opinion if you wish.

Please sign and return this agreement.

Very truly yours,

Signed   Accepted

Date   Date:

Sample agreement

Rejecting the case. You can turn down a case for any reason: time, inclination or conflict of interests. You do not want to go to trial for a losing side. You do not even want to appear in court for the winning side in a bad case. Both will detract from your professional reputation.

Be objective and take a case only if you are on the side of right. If the case is a poor one, inform your client-attorney. He or she probably will not want you to continue on the case. Sometimes, client-attorneys attempt to proceed with an expert who does not support their case. Most experts will drop out in such situations.

Do not accept a case for which you are not qualified. You will probably be found out and embarrassed. The woods are full of rent-an-experts and opposing attorneys love to tear them apart in court.

If you make your investigation and find you cannot support the client-attorney's position, say so (orally) and recommend that you stop working on the case. Submit your bill but do not send a written report unless it is requested.

If you cannot be wholehearted about your testimony, turn down the case. It is better to turn down a case and lose the business than to do a poor job or lose your self-respect.

If the prospective client-attorney appears to be careless, uncooperative or disreputable, reject the case. You want to work with professionals who will enhance your reputation, not someone who will injure it.

If you turn down or later excuse yourself from a case, the file should remain confidential. Return all the materials furnished by the client-attorney by certified mail, return receipt. Keep a list of the items returned.

Once you reject a case, list the reasons in your folder and file the folder. Then do not talk to anyone else about the case; it may not be ethical.

February 30, 1988

Lunch v. Dinner
Certified mail - return receipt

Dear Mr. Lyon:

I am unable to serve as an expert witness in the above referenced case (do not say why) and am returning the documents and the unused portion of the retainer.

Please keep my name on file. I hope you will contact me when you next have a case in my area of expertise.

Very truly yours,

Sample letter rejecting case

Switching sides. If you turn down a case in which you have done more than read the complaint, other public documents and a cover letter, it is not ethical to work for the other side. Some courts have ruled it impermissible to hire an expert previously engaged by the other side.

If you do turn down a case and are then contacted by the other side, tell the calling attorney of your prior involvement in the case. He or she will have to decide whether you are free to switch and how to answer the inevitable questions in court. Make sure the calling attorney wants to hire you, and that he or she is not just fishing for information.

It is best to ask only for non-confidential information and to insist on an advance payment and contract before starting work. Until you accept the advance and take the case, you are free to negotiate with the other side. If you do not follow these suggestions, you may find yourself unable to serve either side.

Conflict of interests. There are times when you should not take a case because you are too close to it. Even if you do not feel too close, a judge or jury might think otherwise. On the other hand, there are times when similarities in your condition (you have suffered an injury similar to the plaintiff's) or experience may work in your favor. A conflict may also arise if you have done business or have otherwise been associated with (friend, relative, etc.) the plaintiff, defendant, other attorneys or anyone associated with the case. Whenever there is a potential conflict, let your client-attorney know.

Q: *You served on the board of the association for sixteen years; then wouldn't you say you are protective of the association and are inclined to defend the sport and the industry?*

A: *Yes, I am protective of the sport and industry. I have a reputation for being very straight-laced. Whenever I see misconduct, I point it out to the proper authority. The best way to protect the sport and the industry is to make sure every manufacturer and school is operating with proper quality control.*

Record keeping. As soon as you have been contacted and agree to look into a case, set up a file folder. Write the names of the case and the attorney on the top tab.

Cat v. Dog, et. al.   Robert F. Egenolf, Esq.

File folder labeling

Write the attorney's name and telephone number on the inside of the folder so that they will be easy to find. Keep a running time sheet in the folder. Place all correspondence, your narrative and other documents there. If you receive an especially large stack of depositions, they may have to be placed in a separate folder and/or stored elsewhere, but place a note showing their location in the folder. Some experts like to maintain separate files for time and billing, research, and correspondence. This system separates the administrative material from the opinion material. Another way to handle larger cases is to transfer the contents of the folder to a two- or three-inch accordion file. Some cases may require three-ring binders.

Support documents such as photographs, copies of regulations, position papers, and articles will also go into this file folder.

Keep records of all work. Every time you receive a call from your client-attorney or otherwise spend time on the case, note the following on a fresh sheet of paper: date, time started and stopped, and a brief description of the work. Your running time sheet and these notes will be the basis for billing the client.

Do not discard the file once the case is complete. Make a brief summary of the disposition of the case and place it in front of the file folder. You may need the information again or you may be asked about it in a subsequent case.

Accounting. Since expert witness work requires written reports, a word processor is almost mandatory. The computer also enables you to maintain records for your consulting business. Bicycle expert John Forester has designed the Small Consultant's Accounting program to operate on the IBM Personal Computer (and workalikes). For details, contact him at 726 Madrone Avenue, Suite 401, Sunnyvale, CA 94086.

Travel records are most easily kept on a plain #10 envelope. Take a standard business envelope, cut open the end and seal the top flap. As you travel to depositions and trial, note all your expenditures on the outside of the envelope. Write down what you spend each day for meals and lodging, air and other fares, travel expenses such as cabs and tips, and so on. Place any receipts you receive in the envelope. When you return home, you will have a detailed record of every penny spent and you will be ready to bill the client and enter the information into your own ledger.

Continuing correspondence. Every three to six months, review all your open cases and write to each client-attorney. Ask if the case is still active, if a court date has been set and if you should keep the file open. Some cases drag on for years.

Follow-up correspondence. Sending a letter to a client-attorney after a case has been resolved is just good public relations. Obviously, the letter is easier to write if your side won. But if you lost, he or she feels badly, too. Your letter could cheer up the client-attorney. In any case, this attorney may have business for you in the future or may recommend you to fellow attorneys. Build bridges, do not burn them.

CHAPTER FOUR

Opinion Forming

As a technical witness you are not hired to *give* an opinion. You are hired to *arrive* at an opinion after thorough investigation. There is a subtle but essential difference.

The opposing attorney may try to trap you by asking when you formed your opinion. He or she may try to show that you agreed to testify before studying the case adequately. Defending yourself will be easier if you can show you read every applicable document (the complaint, interrogatories, depositions, test reports), ran tests, inspected the equipment, visited the site, performed library research, and spoke with witnesses and other experts before committing yourself to an opinion.

The expert *interprets* scientific and technological facts and *renders* scientific and technological opinions based on the facts. Opinions must be based on fact and scientific probability. Do not give opinions unless you can provide information to support them.

The facts on which an expert's opinion is based must come from:

1. Personal observation of the facts. Whatever you saw in your investigation

2. Personal knowledge of the particular field. What you have learned about this subject area through education, experience or training

3. Assumed facts supported by evidence admitted in the case.

Do your best to get all the facts, whether they support your case or not. You want to see the entire file on the case. Be persistent and continue to request any information you need to form an opinion. Some attorneys will hold back on evidence damaging to the case. Your opinion could change when presented with omitted facts during cross-examination. It is better for all concerned if you have all the facts before the trial begins.

Client-attorneys cannot know as much about your subject as you do. They do not even understand the relevance of some of the material they have. Make sure you get to see everything, even information they think is not important.

You can't get too much information. Once you have read the complaint and interrogatories, draft a list of questions that need answers. List the tests you must run and the research you must do. Many times, experts do not form opinions until the case is well underway.

One reason your client-attorney might hold back information is that he or she is afraid the other side will find it in your file during discovery. Your files are open; the attorney's are not.

Form an opinion on what you know and do not venture out of your area. It is far better to limit your testimony or even to give up the job than to represent yourself as an expert in unknown territory.

One line of questioning went as follows:

Q: *When did you form your opinion?*
A: *The day before yesterday.*
Q: *The day before the trial started?*
A: *Yes. The problem was that the plaintiff would not allow me to inspect the subject equipment. This forced me to run many, many tests to try out several theories. After the September 28th visit to the factory and the tests performed there, I had a fairly firm impression as to the cause. I could not confirm that theory until I saw the equipment on January 12th. Yes, this would have put the defendant in a very difficult position if I had not seen what I thought I would see.*

Before going to a deposition or into court, review your notes to refresh your memory concerning when your opinion was actually formed. It may be helpful to write out a time/event schedule similar to the one which follows. With this time-line to refresh your memory before you go into court, you will be able to rattle off the dates of each event.

When I formed my opinion

January 26, 1987: Peter Levin called me. He also mentioned the case a couple of times at national conventions. He wanted to tie me up (preferably on his side.)

May 13, 1987: John Moore of Moore and Moore called me.

May 15, 1987: I sent my CV, rates, etc. to Moore.

August 31, 1987: Jones contacted me. See my deposition, page 11.

September 1-8, 1987: I conducted research. Read depositions to date, used own library and called other experts.

September 8, 1987: Memo to the factory regarding tests to be run.

September 13-14, 1987: Trip to the factory to see the quality control system, discover paperwork in files, and run tests.

September 15, 1987: I wrote Jones asking to investigate the equipment.

September 28, 1987: Trip to the factory to run tests, etc.

January 12, 1988: Inspected equipment for first time and confirmed suspicions.

Formed opinion.

February 16, 1988: I was deposed.

Opinion forming chronology

CHAPTER FIVE

Case Preparation

- Working with the Client-Attorney
- Oral and Written Reports

Your client-attorney is in charge of the case. While you are a member of the team, he or she calls the plays. It is not your job to change a play or take control. You could be doing something not in the game plan. Remember: expert witnesses do not win or lose cases. They assist attorneys who win or lose cases.

Your job is one of *service*. Do not tell the client-attorney your problems. He or she wants to know what information you can offer, and is paying you to solve problems. The attorney wants your best opinion based on your knowledge, experience, research and tests.

You specialize in *objectively* analyzing failures and advising attorneys so they may prepare their case. They may point out important information or angles to you, while you may alert them to topics they shouldn't address.

Keep the relationship with your client-attorney on a professional level to avoid becoming an advocate.

Your role before the trial. You are a consultant to your client-attorney. Before the trial, you may assist in:

- Educating the client-attorney

- Suggesting sources of evidence

- Helping draft interrogatories and interpreting answers

- Investigating and testing

- Preparing deposition questions

- Helping prepare the other witnesses

- Preparing (advising and consulting) exhibits and demonstrative evidence

- Suggesting case strategy.

A case calendar could look like this:

1. Attorney calls expert, determines qualifications, briefly describes case, asks if the expert is interested and requests a first impression.

2. Expert mails curriculum vita, fee schedule and other materials with a cover letter to attorney.

3. Attorney writes expert a letter enclosing a copy of the complaint, witness statements, photographs and a check. Expert opens a file on the case.

4. Expert reviews materials, drafts narrative and calls attorney with a preliminary opinion and requests more information and documentation. Expert may have several questions.

5. Attorney sends requested materials to expert.

6. Expert writes attorney requesting authorization to conduct further research and tests. Costs are estimated.

7. Attorney authorizes research and tests.

8. Attorney asks expert to draft some interrogatories to be sent to the opposing side, for both the opposing expert and the other opposing parties.

9. Attorney asks expert to help answer interrogatories received from the opposition. Expert drafts a formal written opinion.

10. Attorney informs expert he will be deposed by the other side. They discuss the case, anticipate difficult questions and attend the deposition.

11. Attorney asks expert to attend the deposition of the opposing expert to counsel attorney. This rarely happens.

12. Attorney asks expert to attend a settlement conference to advise him or her. This rarely happens.

13. Attorney and expert prepare for the trial. Demonstrative evidence in the form of models and charts are constructed. Both review testimony and anticipate difficult cross-examination questions. Courtroom demonstrations are rehearsed for clarity and flow.

14. Expert testifies at trial.

15. Expert writes follow-up letter to attorney and closes file.

Maintain close contact with your client-attorney. Call periodically to check on the status of the case. Inform each other of what you find and what you learn. Work with your client-attorney to schedule depositions and the trial around your calendar.

Be professional. Your image as an expert is affected by your promotional materials and advertising, your initial meeting with the attorney (he or she is sizing you up), how you brief the client-attorney on your findings, the appearance and tone of your written report, and your testimony.

Witness list. In most jurisdictions, expert witnesses must be named before the trial. The amount of time *may* be at least 70 days before the trial starts but at least ten days after the setting of the trial date. Rules vary from jurisdiction to jurisdiction. Witnesses not on the list are barred from testifying. This window of time is necessary to make the expert witnesses available for depositions.

To notify the opposing side that you are on the case, your client-attorney will write them a letter. The letter will list your name, address, a brief statement on your qualifications and the general substance of your anticipated testimony.

Investigating the opposing expert witness. The opposing side will send a similar witness list to your client-attorney. Your side will want to know who the opposing expert will be and what his or her opinion is going to be. You will study the position of the opposing expert and advise your client-attorney on courses of action. Normally you will be in a better position to investigate and evaluate an opposing witness than your client-attorney. If your field is narrow, you will probably know the opposing expert.

Both you and your client-attorney will want to know:

• The length of time the opposing expert has worked as a litigation consultant

• The number and identity of cases in which he or she was involved

• His or her balance of cases. How many times has he or she worked for the plaintiff and defense. Is this expert really objective or does he or she favor one side?

• Did any of these previous cases involve the same issues? How many cases and which ones?

• Has this expert ever worked for this law firm before?

• Has this expert performed litigation consulting for this client before?

• Has this expert ever worked for his or her client in any other (regular) capacity?

• What percentage of the expert's time is spent in the field and what percentage as a litigation consultant?

• Request a copy of the expert's curriculum vita. What is his or her background?

• What has the expert published? Where can copies be obtained?

- Does the expert have any experience *particularly* relevant to the subject?

Some of the above questions will be answered through your investigation. Others will require interrogatories or deposition questions. Advise your client-attorney of the questions you need answered.

What do you know about the opposing experts? How are they perceived by your peers? Have they been involved in any controversies? Are there any skeletons in their closet? Is there anything that might tarnish their reputations? How can they be expected to react to certain questions?

Narrative. A *narrative* is a summary of what happened. It includes the names of the parties, date and place of the accident, basic events, weather, injuries, etc. Every time you discover new material, update or correct it. Review the narrative and all the written material in your file before you give a deposition or go to trial. Second readings of the file will reveal ideas and facts overlooked in your initial reading. Start building a narrative listing only the facts (no opinions) of the case on your word processor. As you read depositions and other materials, add to the narrative.

The layout of narratives will vary depending on the type of case. Some accident cases may follow this outline:

Plaintiff: name, age, height, weight, marital status, dependents, employer, name of attorney and firm

Defendant: name, age, height, weight, marital status, dependents, employer, name of attorney and firm

Date and place of accident

Weather conditions

Training/experience

Equipment

Events

Injuries

Allegations

Defenses

Schedule for deposition, trial, etc.

Layout of narrative

The narrative is kept on top of your file folder. It may be used for quick review any time you need to refresh your memory on the case.

Unless you have misunderstood a material fact, it does not hurt to let the opposition discover your narrative. But, make sure your client-attorney has reviewed it for accuracy.

Attorneys often call with questions about the case when you haven't looked at the file for several months. These calls can result in embarrassment and even a lost client if you forget the facts and which side you are on and start supplying arguments which do not support this attorney's case. Just say: *I am busy with (a client, etc); let me call you back in fifteen minutes.* Then go read the file and narrative before returning the call.

A narrative also proves you have done your work. It can be matched to time sheets should you ever have to justify a billing to your client-attorney.

Investigate and report findings. Keep written correspondence to a minimum. Once you have agreed to testify, your entire file becomes discoverable. See Chapter Eight.

Oral reports. Your initial report to your client-attorney will probably be oral. If you are in the same town, the report may be made in person. If you are some distance apart, the report will be made over the telephone. Many attorneys ask their expert not to submit a written report until all the facts of the case have been discovered. They do not want the expert's opinion to be impeached by a report based on antiquated or false information. Further, the attorney does not want your opinion committed to paper until he or she knows what it is.

Orally list the strengths and weaknesses of the case. Tell the client-attorney where you think the case stands.

Here is a procedure for controlling your telephone bills when providing oral reports. Try to call before eight or after five (depending on your time zone) and ask to speak to the client-attorney's secretary. Identify yourself and the case and ask to have the attorney call you for a report *at his or her convenience.* This three-minute call will be very inexpensive. The lengthy return call will be on the attorney's bill.

Written reports. Your client-attorney may request a written report. It can be a brief letter on the cause of the accident, an expanded letter explaining your opinion or a full-blown lengthy tome in a report cover.

In some states, New Jersey for example, a written report is not only required, it is supplied to the jury.

Your client-attorney will ask for a thorough report if the intent is to settle the case, and a simple report if the intent is to go to court. In the latter case, he or she will not want to give your position away completely.

The formal report notifies the attorneys on both sides of the expert's opinion. It is assumed that trial testimony will be the same. It is possible, however, that new information will cause an expert to alter his or her opinion. If you find yourself in this situation, you should notify your client-attorney immediately and probably draft a superseding report.

If you send a draft of a report to your client-attorney, mark it *draft*. You do not want readers to think, or be able to say, it is a final opinion.

Always discuss the probable contents of your written report with your client-attorney before committing your opinion to paper. Understand the purpose of the report and what is necessary to it. Many adverse parties may see your work before the case is eventually closed.

Since some 97% of cases never go to trial, your written report could cause the plaintiff to drop the case or the defendant to settle. Your written report is also the cornerstone of your courtroom presentation.

The longer you wait to prepare your written report, the more information you will have. Opinions and positions can change in light of new information. Additionally, some experts find it emotionally difficult to retreat from an earlier conclusive position.

Your report should be impartial, objective and thorough. Avoid statements the other side could pretend to misinterpret in court. List other experts, articles, and books you consulted. Cite all scientific tests that support your conclusion. List the machinery, test equipment, gauges, standards and test methods used. Render technically correct statements in all communication. All your written documents will be compared so make sure interrogatories, depositions and written reports agree. Do not misrepresent the facts upon which you base your opinion. You will be caught.

Your report should look professional. Use a word processor with laser or letter-quality printer and good paper. The *full-blown lengthy report* should have a cover sheet with a title, citing the case, your name and address and the client-attorney's name and address. Inside, describe the accident or problem, the reports and other reference materials, site visits and equipment you relied on. Discuss the problems and state your conclusion. Diagrams, photos or photocopies might be appended. Include a cover letter reciting the transmission of the report. Recheck your spelling.

Write clearly. A non-expert reader must be able to understand what you are saying. Do not send out a report the same day you write it. Sleep on it, review it and revise it as needed.

CHAPTER SIX

Position Papers

Writing a position paper helps you review the case and clarify your thoughts. If the opposing attorney asks you to cite the relative merits of the flat circular and conical parachute canopies, you want to be able to rattle off the comparative advantages and disadvantages without hesitation. The faster you can rattle them off, the more credible you will appear and the more uneasy the opposing attorney will feel about cross-examining you.

Researching and writing the position paper helps you get your facts straight and identify any problem areas. Type up the information and put the draft in a file folder with photocopies of all the supporting reference material (magazine articles, military specifications, maps, etc.).

Position papers may also become scholarly answers to important questions in your field. They may be used as the basis for magazine articles, becoming another source of income; while being published validates your expertise and your theory. Then, next time you need the information in court, you may even cite your own article.

Position papers on the same general subject area may be the basis for a book. Books validate your expertise even better than magazine articles.

Do not, however, write an article or book on the subject of a case until the case is concluded. Your attorney may not want you to reveal your thoughts or information sources. This secrecy can create a difficult problem for experts. What if your investigation reveals a safety problem? Shouldn't you spread the word as quickly and widely as possible?

For now, research, write and bank your material. Over the years as the files take shape, you will think of other ways to use the information.

Position papers are a product of your research done on billable time. This study makes you a better expert, and the material can be used again. Repackaging the information provides more income, while the article, book, video or lecture can be listed in your CV as evidence of your expertise.

CHAPTER SEVEN

Maintaining Competence

It is important to remember that you are a consultant in your field of expertise, not a professional expert witness. Do not let expert witness activity overshadow your original line of work. Keep up-to-date on what is happening in your field.

In some areas of expertise (document examination and criminal laboratory work, for examples) you are actually practicing your technical skill when you act as an expert witness. But, most experts have to maintain their competence by continuing to work in their field because, when testifying, they are evaluating the skills of others rather than honing their own.

Maryland has passed a law requiring that experts spend a minimum of 80% of their professional *time* in their area of expertise. Kansas has a 50% rule, and bills are pending in other states. The object of these laws is to make sure witnesses are experts, not just courtroom performers.

Most attorneys prefer expert witnesses with some courtroom experience. New witnesses may appear less contaminated but they are less predictable. Attorneys like street-wise experts they can count on. These experts are much easier to prepare for deposition and trial.

Opposing counsel may try to show that you are a hired gun, a professional expert witness, by asking what percentage of your business comes from being an expert witness. You must answer these questions truthfully but you can turn them to your advantage. You may spend 10% of your time on this kind of work while it may constitute 40% of your gross income.

Q: *What percentage of your income is from expert witness work?*
A: *I spend about 10% of my time advising lawyers and educating juries.*

Q: *When did you race last?*
A: *It has been almost five years. In the last race, I suffered a major accident and was laid up for over a year. I am not able to race now.*
   (You show you would still be active if you were able and you turn a difficult situation into one where you gain sympathy from the jury.)

Q: *When did you last exercise your license to _____ ?*
A: *Two hours ago.*
   (At this point he or she may be too cautious to go on.)
Q: *You mean you were out _____ .*
A: *No, according to the regulations, exercising one's license could be interpreted as working hands-on with the equipment, reading a manual or teaching a class.*

There are many ways to measure professional time. You are certainly not on vacation when you attend conferences, write a magazine article or read professional magazines. Since you probably work more than eight hours each day and 40 hours each week, it would not be fair to compute your activity with those numbers.

Keep all of these views in mind and anticipate the inevitable questions regarding your maintenance of competence.

You do not want to become a professional expert witness. Your client should be truth, not the side that hired you. If you spend all your time in court, you will establish a negative credential as a full-time expert.

CHAPTER EIGHT

Discovery of Evidence and Your Files

Discovery is a set of procedures which allows any party to the dispute to obtain information bearing on the case.

The objectives of pre-trial discovery are to locate evidence (and preserve all relevant material for use at the trial), preserve testimony, narrow the issues (to avoid spending court time on undisputed facts), remove surprise and promote settlement. The forms of discovery are interrogatories, production of documents and things, requests for admission, physical and mental (medical) examinations, oral depositions, and depositions by means of written interrogatories.

Just as your client-attorney wants to know your opinion and what you base it on, your opponent attorney wants to know too. Opposing counsel will normally use interrogatories and/or a deposition proceeding to determine your opinion.

Interrogatories are lists of questions drafted by one side and sent to the other. The object of interrogatories is to go fishing for helpful information. Consequently, the other side often tries to answer unimportant questions fully and important questions vaguely. You and your attorney will probably work together on any interrogatories presented to your side.

In Federal proceedings, interrogatories are normally used to identify the experts, to reveal the subject matter on which they are expected to testify, and to state the substance of the facts and opinions on which the expert plans to testify. Just knowing the expert's area of expertise (ballistics, psychology, handwriting) can tell you a lot about your opponent's approach to the case.

Attorney-client privilege. New expert witnesses are often shocked to find their files are not private. The *attorney-client relationship* of confidentiality does not protect your files from the opposing attorney. Only the plaintiff or defendant who has hired the attorney to obtain legal advice has this relationship. On the other hand, if the client-plaintiff or client-defendant reveals confidential information to the expert in order to help the expert form an opinion to relay to the attorney, there may be an attorney-client privilege.

An expert who is also an employee of the client-plaintiff or client-defendant has been held to be an extension of the client and protected by the attorney-client privilege.

Attorney work product. *Attorney work product* is not discoverable but your work may not be protected by this rule. *Work product* is limited to material prepared by an attorney as an attorney and usually refers only to his or her notes, analysis and trial strategy.

There are two reasons for the work product rule: 1. To encourage counsel to thoroughly prepare both favorable and unfavorable parts of the case and 2. to prevent one attorney from taking advantage of the other's industry and efforts.

Information you record as a consultant *prior* to being retained for the trial is usually considered part of your client-attorney's work product which is not discoverable. This is because your advice is part of his or her research. You must be acting as an associate of the attorney in the preparation of a confidential report to be used by the attorney. This is one reason why many attorneys request that you make your first report orally, over the telephone.

The rules change when you graduate from consultant to witness. Once you have been retained for the trial, whatever you have in your file is discoverable — even your earlier work. This is because the other side has a right to know your position (opinion).

One case held that information given by the expert to the attorney is work product but that any information not given to the attorney is discoverable. Certainly if you are being paid directly by the attorney's client, the work you do cannot be considered attorney work product.

Information communicated by the client-attorney to the expert witness may be privileged if the information is necessary for the expert to to accomplish his or her job. If your client-attorney steers your investigation in the proper direction, the communication may not be discoverable.

To obtain maximum protection from the work product rule, the client-attorney should retain you and all your work should be transmitted directly to the client-attorney. If you have already been hired by the client, counsel should write you a letter retaining you directly.

For the sake of confidentiality, attorneys often like to put off naming their experts as long as possible.

Discoverability. Once you are designated a witness to testify at the trial, the work product rule is waived and all earlier communications become discoverable. Since anything in writing is easily discoverable, many experts consolidate their files and destroy their notes once they have been declared a witness. They reduce their files to useful reports only.

Some experts go further and purge their file of all negative material. Judges and lawyers know that files are often sanitized and frequently overlook this fact. The best rule is not to commit any thought to paper that could hurt you if read by the other side. While you must always answer truthfully when testifying, you do not have to provide the opposition with a written record of potentially damaging information.

Today, many experts keep their information in their computer. Their documents become ever-growing files; they make changes and delete the irrelevant.

Q: *Where are your earlier notes?*
A: *That earlier material was written over. With a computer, you do not save scraps of paper.*

The above interpretations are generalities. Remember that lawyers deal in exceptions. When in doubt about attorney-client relationship rules, work product and discoverability, consult your client-attorney. The safest rule is simply to treat everything as discoverable.

Protection. You may ask for a court order to protect sensitive documents in your file (proprietary formulas, income figures, etc.). That is, you will still have to turn them over to the opposing attorney, but he or she may not show them to anyone.

Some items in your file such as books and magazines may be covered by copyright. When copies are requested, remind opposing counsel that photocopying them may violate copyright law.

Be careful of the question: *What documents have you reviewed?* Any records, photographs, books, etc. you have seen can be requested by the other side.

Sometimes the opposing attorney tries to harass the expert by using a subpoena duces tecum to request all of his or her files — he or she wants to see every case ever worked on and the expert's entire library. If this happens to you, call your client-attorney to try and have the subpoena modified or withdrawn. If the requesting attorney is firm, quote a price to cover time and photocopying costs. Request payment in advance. You are entitled to do this but you must provide an itemized statement of your work. Faced with a large bill, the attorney may back off.

Record retention. You must retain your files, exhibits and other evidence until the case is completely settled. That is until after the time for appeal has expired. Waiting a year after final settlement is usually sufficient, but many experts save everything as they may be able to use the materials again. Consult with your client-attorney before disposing of any materials.

CHAPTER NINE

Demonstrative Evidence

Demonstrative evidence is an exhibit which supports expert opinion. Properly designed, it shows what your opinion is and how you arrived at it.

Demonstrative evidence can be anything that appeals to the jury's senses: sight, touch, smell, taste, or hearing. It may include models, diagrams, charts, photographs, videos, maps, and so on. Designed to inform, persuade, justify and educate, it can be used to help the jury focus on the critical issues of the case.

Remember the maxim among educators: people will remember 10% of what they hear, 20% of what they see, 50% of what they read, and 90% of what they do. Involve your jury! Demonstrative evidence has a wake–up effect. It can be used to refocus the attention of an otherwise bored jury. Studies show they will remember 65% of a demonstrative presentation after 72 hours while retaining only 10% of oral testimony alone. And you can leave the drawings up to make a continuous impression. Even better, demonstrative evidence goes into the jury room when they deliberate. Yes, a picture is worth a thousand words.

Your client-attorney may ask you to obtain models or other demonstrative evidence. You do not have to physically prepare the exhibits yourself but you do have to *direct the preparation.* Since the exhibits are presented to demonstrate your theories, they should be *your* exhibits. The opposing attorney will ask if you prepared them.

Professional exhibit makers. There are firms that specialize in designing and manufacturing courtroom exhibits (see the *Yellow Pages*). They can turn your sketches into professional presentations.

One benefit of working with professional exhibit people is that in explaining what you want and working over the development of the exposition, you become much more familiar with your own work. You will learn more about the case, while the preparation will help you to focus on your theories and opinions.

Types of exhibits:

1. Photographs can make a case seem more real, especially *before–and–after* shots. Photographs may be of equipment, the site, or the plaintiff.

Photographs taken by the expert carry far more weight than those taken by a professional photographer. Viewers may suspect the professional took the photos in a way that slants the subject. Additionally, your photos show you were there and studied the subject or the site.

Photographs need only be an *accurate portrayal* of what they are supposed to represent. The type of camera and film are not important, even though opposing attorneys sometimes try to discount photographs taken with inexpensive cameras. On the other hand, the technical details may become important if the photograph is being used to demonstrate dimensions.

2. Videotape offers the advantage of motion. It can also be stopped and replayed. Jurors are generally comfortable with video today as most use it in their own lives.

Video is being used more and more in the courtroom and as tool a to encourage settlement. To be effective, however, it must be a true and accurate representation of something the jury needs to know.

Many attorneys are videotaping depositions, especially when they have reason to believe the witness might not be available to testify at the trial.

If you are using a film projector, slide projector, video player, etc., bring your own and test it in the courtroom before the trial.

3. Charts and graphs are most effective for clarifying your case or opinion.

It is best to present just one message per chart. Multiple ideas can be confusing.

Some experts like to use Mylar overlays with separating sheets of paper. This system allows them to build their presentation while saving their conclusion for the finish. Mylar also allows you to write on the exhibit without obliterating it.

Stand on the left side of the easel and do not block it. Encourage the jury to look at your drawing and then let their eyes drift back to you. Make sure the evidence can be seen; consider size and position.

4. Diagrams are most effectively used in augmenting witness testimony. They work particularly well when used in conjunction with other visual aids such as photographs.

Take your own marker pens—several different colors—to court. Do not expect all the equipment to be there. Use the black marker pens first. They are easier to read. If the opposing side has already used black, select a color that is readily distinguishable from theirs. Some experts like to use water-based markers with Handi-wipes to allow for erasures.

5. Maps may be used to establish locations and distances.

6. X-rays, medical illustrations and anatomical models can be very useful in injury cases.

7. Three-dimensional models are good for recreating accident sites. Operational models are often useful in patent infringement cases.

8. Courtroom demonstrations of a procedure can backfire, so do not use them unless you are certain of the outcome. Go through the demonstrations several times and get a critique. Your best critic may be a professional court exhibit maker. Make sure your demonstration shows what you want the jury to understand. Committing the experiment to video tape is safer. You can repeat the procedure until you get the results you want.

9. Documents. When letters and other documents are discussed, it is often wise to provide copies for the judge and each juror. Important words or passages may be accented with a highlighting pen. The impact will be greater if each can hold the document in his or her hands. If you want to point to important areas, you may use a blow-up of the let-

ter. Blow-ups may appear more important than smaller documents when taken into the jury room.

Do not over-do it. Too much demonstrative evidence can be confusing and may be likened to a three-ring circus. Present the case to the jury in the most graphic way without being over-dramatic.

Do not make your demonstrative evidence look too expensive. Do not trot out huge glossy photographs when simple snapshots will do. Viewers may become suspicious if your side is spending money on exhibits that the case does not appear to warrant.

On the other hand, some attorneys are reluctant to spend any money on demonstrative evidence. You must explain what you need and counsel against going into court with the second–best models and drawings. Be assertive or creative. Come up with less-expensive alternatives.

Check the layout of the courtroom and your distance from the jury. Make your exhibits large enough to be easily seen but small enough to fit through the door. Scout the sizes of the elevators, stairways and entryways.

Keep your drawings and models covered until ready for presentation. Build the jury's curiosity; do not distract them during earlier testimony.

Exhibits go with the jurors into the jury room, so think carefully about what you want to leave with them. Your models and drawings will speak for you long after the jurors forget what you said. Some experts like to use marker pens and large sheets of paper for *chalk talks*, drawing as they explain. But, they may be stopped before making their full presentation and their drawings may not be professional.

Pre-drawn exhibits are already complete and will give the jury the whole story.

Always practice with your models. Get a critique on your presentation. You want to communicate your opinion accurately. The opposing attorney will use your models or drawings against you if he or she can.

To get demonstrative material entered into evidence, have your attorney expose it at a pretrial conference. At trial he or she can say *But your honor, he saw this three weeks ago and did not object.* Also try to see the opposing expert's demonstrative evidence prior to trial so that you can check it for accuracy.

Before preparing an exhibit, consider the foundational criteria and its admissibility.

1. Foundational criteria.

a. Demonstrative evidence must be accurate and to scale. The opposing attorney will ask you about accuracy.

b. Was it built under your direction and can you verify that it is a correct representation? Have you signed and dated it?

c. Will it help to explain and verify your verbal testimony?

d. Are you sure it will not mislead the jury?

e. Are you qualified to testify as to the accuracy of the exhibit?

2. Admissibility.

a. The judge will rule on the admissibility of your demonstrative evidence. If your model, drawing, video, etc. will help the jury to understand the problem, the judge will let the jury see it. If the judge feels your design is misleading, he or she will not.

b. Is the exhibit accurate?

c. Is the exhibit relevant and material?

Once admitted, exhibits will be marked for identification by the court stenographer. Normally, exhibits are marked sequentially and are preceded by a "P" or "D" depending on whether they have been introduced by the plaintiff or defendant. Once marked, the exhibit becomes part of the record.

CHAPTER TEN

The Deposition

A deposition is a form of oral testimony taken by the opposing attorney in advance of the trial. As a notary public, the court reporter places the witness under oath so that testimony is given under penalty of perjury. Then as a certified stenographer, he or she records the testimony.

Notice of deposition. Both your client-attorney and the opposing attorney will probably call you to arrange a convenient time and place for the deposition. It is not unusual, however, for the opposing attorney to formally subpoena you. If you are served, notify your client-attorney immediately.

Failure to appear. If you should fail to show up for the deposition, your absence could prove to be expensive — both for you and the other parties. If your failure to appear is *willful,* you can be held in contempt of court, a charge that could result in your being fined and imprisoned. The opposing attorney will also have a claim against you for out-of-pocket expenses and perhaps even his or her fees for time spent attending the abortive deposition, at hourly rates of $100 to $300. Further, if you fail to appear for the deposition, the judge will probably bar you from testifying at the trial. If you do not wish to be deposed, seek advice from your client-attorney.

You will not be deposed in every case. The opposing attorney has to decide if questioning you is worth the time and money.

If you are serving only as a consultant to your client-attorney and have not been named to testify in court, you will not be deposed. Opinions of, and work by, consultants are covered by the attorney work product rule.

Depositions have two purposes: discovery and/or impeachment. They allow the opposing attorney to examine you under conditions less formal but no less important than a trial. The form of the questions will reveal the opposing attorney's major interest. If discovery is the goal, the questions will be broad and the subjects far-reaching. He or she will be looking for new facts. If the questions are tightly focused, he or she is trying to produce admissible evidence for the trial. The object is to force you to commit yourself to a position. Your client-attorney *may* follow with questions to clarify certain areas.

1. **Discovery** is a fishing expedition to learn new facts, so do not volunteer information. The opposing attorney's objective is to get you to help in his or her research. The opposing attorney wants to know to whom you talked, what you read, what tests you ran, what investigations you made, your research and findings. In other words, the opposing attorney is trying to *discover* how you arrived at your opinion to see what kind of a case your side has. He or she wants to know what work you have done on the case, what you plan to do and what position you are taking.

2. **Impeachment** is designed to nail down your testimony for use at trial. The opposing attorney wants to find what your case will be. The object of the deposition is to reveal and test your opinions and conclusions and to pin you down to them. Be prepared: anticipate questions. If you make a mistake in the deposition, you will pay for it in court.

The opposing attorney may read a sentence from your deposition, and ask *Did you say that?* Then he or she will ask *Do you still agree with that?* and then will ask you to justify what you said in light of some other evidence. Juries tend not to believe witnesses who change their story.

Q: *Did you lie in your deposition, or are you lying now?*

The opposing attorney should be so well prepared for the deposition that he or she knows the subject of your expertise and is fairly sure of your answers. Generally, if the deposition is short, the opposing attorney is good. If it is long and has a number of semi-relevant questions, the attorney has not done his or her homework.

Normally only one deposition is taken of an expert witness. Unless the case is very large, you are not liable to be deposed more than once.

Preparation for the deposition. The opposition has a right to depose you and you cannot be properly deposed unless you are prepared. If you cannot answer the questions, the deposition will be meaningless and the opposition may move to have you barred from testifying at the trial. They may even get a court order making you pay their fees and expenses because you were not prepared for the deposition.

Insist on a lengthy conference with your client-attorney in advance of the deposition. Rehearse by posing the same questions either of you expect the opposing attorney to ask. You must work together and be ready with concisely-framed answers. Too many busy attorneys meet with their experts for only half an hour or so, often over a hurried breakfast. This is not enough time.

Request a briefing on the law relevant to the action. You want to know how your testimony fits into the case.

You will also be asked about your qualifications. The opposing attorney hopes to expose potential bias or lack of qualifications.

Tell your client-attorney if you have ever expressed a contrary opinion in a previous case, a magazine article or book. How long ago was it? Has thinking, teaching or equipment changed? How can you justify a change of thought now?

Be prepared and read everything. Remember, some 97% of cases never go to trial—the plaintiff gives up or the defendant makes a settlement. Therefore, you must win in the deposition. Be ready to rattle off all the things you did and read before forming an opinion. Do not try to wing it. If you are sure of your material, you need not feel threatened.

What to wear. Wear whatever you wear on the job. Be comfortable, be clean and neat. Men should usually wear a suit or conservative jacket and tie. Similarly, women should dress for business. You want to give the impression that you are a serious, quiet, careful, thoughtful individual. Remember, the opposing attorney will be sizing you up. He or she will be evaluating how you will act in court.

What to take. Take only your file folder with CV, fee schedule, narrative, time sheets, bills, reports, and backup documents. You should have all facts and data upon which you relied in forming your opinion, but take only what you want the other side to know. Anything in your file is discoverable. Show the file to your attorney in the meeting prior to the deposition. He or she will want to filter out all non-discoverable (privileged) information. The opposing attorney may ask the stenographer to photocopy the entire file and attach it to the deposition.

Take demonstrative evidence such as models or drawings if they will help to explain your case.

Do not allow depositions to be taken at your home or business. Anything you have with you is discoverable and if you are at home, all your files are open to the opposing attorney. Suggest a neutral site such as a court reporter's office downtown.

Although selecting the site for the deposition is up to the attorneys, you may have to help if you want to keep them off your premises. Get out the *Yellow Pages* and look up some local court reporting services under *Reporters-Court*. Call two or three for a description of services and rates. Keep this list handy so that when an opposing attorney calls to arrange a deposition, you will be ready with a telephone number he or she may call to secure the site.

The opposing attorney usually begins by asking if you know the ground rules so that you cannot claim at the trial that you did not understand what was going on. Ask the opposing attorney to review the rules even if you have given many depositions. Rules differ from jurisdiction to jurisdiction, and each court changes its rules from time to time. You should not have to research these rules; that is the lawyer's job. You want the record to reflect what the opposing attorney told you. Sample deposition instructions are printed at the end of this chapter.

How to act. Make sure the court reporter understands what you are saying. Talk in complete sentences. Remember, one of the most important considerations in your deposition is this: how will your answers look in writing? You are a teacher. Speak slowly and spell out technical words. When you give your name, spell it out. This is professional and lets the opposing attorney know you have given depositions before. Hand your business card to the court reporter. A card not only assures correct spelling; it lets the reporter know where to send the transcript for review and correction.

If you have taken any medication in the past 48 hours, tell your client-attorney. He or she will want to know if you are not operating at 100% of your capacity.

Be dignified and polite. This is serious, expensive business and you want to project a conscientious image. During the deposition, everything you say will be *on the record*, committed to paper. Do not clown around, even outside the deposition room. The opposing parties may begin to doubt both your sincerity and your testimony. Follow these three basic rules:

1. **Listen to the question and pause before answering it.** The pause permits you to formulate your answer and allows your client-attorney to object to the question if it is improper.

2. **Look directly at the attorney** asking the question and give a responsive answer, but do not volunteer additional information. Carefully phrase your answers and do not add

any unnecessary detail. Remember, the longer the answer, the more likely you are to give away unasked–for information or make an error. Be careful of open-ended questions such as *What happened next?*

3. Tell the complete truth. A deposition is sworn testimony and the transcript can be read into the record at the trial. It is better to say *I do not know* or *I do not remember* than to make a guess.

Q: *Did counsel tell you what to say at this deposition?*
A: *My counsel told me to tell the truth.*

When your client-attorney objects, listen carefully. He or she may be dropping a hint to alert you to a problem area. Whenever your client-attorney starts to talk, stop immediately and listen.

If your client-attorney directs you not to answer a particular question, state *I will not answer on advice of counsel.* Let the attorneys work it out.

Analyze each question. It may be *vague and ambiguous.* Make sure you understand all the terms used. Do not hesitate to ask that the question be reworded. Ask to have words defined so that you are both working with the same meaning. If you do not express a lack of understanding, counsel will presume you understood and your answer will be taken as a full and complete response.

If you think the opposing attorney is trying to be tricky, ask him or her to rephrase the question as a delaying tactic. If the question is ambiguous, make your answer clear and specific.

A: *If you mean..., then the answer is ...*

One effective technique for clarifying the issue is to include the question in your answer.

Q: *When did you run the tests?*
A: *I ran the tensile and tear tests on the fabric on September 17th.*

When a (compound) question has many parts, ask to have it rephrased, one question at a time. Be alert for questions with the words *or* or *and*. Be careful of negative questions; those that start with *is it not true...*

The opposing attorney may ask you a question which does not call for new facts. The question is considered *argumentative* if he or she is seeking an explanation of a previous answer. You may answer with *I have already answered that question.* It is up to your client-attorney to object if the question is argumentative.

Do not make assumptions unless they are based on facts which are in evidence. *Foundation* must exist or your answer will admit the assumed fact.

If the opposing attorney attempts to summarize your testimony, he or she may be *putting words in your mouth* by suggesting things you did not say. Do not accept this characterization of data, assumptions or descriptions of events. Listen carefully and point out each and every inaccurate statement in the summarization.

Leading questions are those with a given statement to which you are only asked to agree. If any part of the question is not correct, you should say that you cannot *entirely* agree.

Hypothetical questions are almost always signs of a mine field. *Assuming this and that and this, what would you expect* *a rational person in this area to do?* Keep your eyes open and tread carefully.

The opposing attorney will look over your curriculum vita and ask some questions about it. Some potentially hazardous questions on items not likely to be covered by your CV are:

1. Your personal relationship with your client-attorney or his/her client. For the answer, see the Trial Chapter.

2. The percentage of your business related to expert witness work. See Chapter Seven on maintaining competence for the answer.

3. The number of times you have testified. How many times for the plaintiff and how many times for the defense? Are you truly objective? Do you have an even balance of cases?

4. The number of times you have been consulted as an expert witness.

5. Your rates of compensation. Hand over your fee schedule. See Chapter Twelve on fees.

6. When you formed your opinion. See Chapter Four on opinion forming for the answer.

If handed a document, take it, identify it and read it very carefully before you answer any questions about it. You could mistake it for some other document.

You will be asked about your research, testing and other preparations for the deposition. This question is similar to the *when–did–you–form–your–opinion* question. You want to show that you thoroughly investigated the situation before forming an opinion. But do not give away too much information since the opposition will scrutinize all your sources.

Catch-all questions. Watch out for statements such as *tell us all you know about...* Make your answer accurate and truthful, but be as brief as possible. Cover yourself by ending with *that is all I can think of at this time.*

Q: *What are your opinions in this case?*
A: *One of my opinions is....,*
   or
A: *I have many opinions on this case. Please specify which aspect of the case you would like my opinion on.*

If you state only a few opinions, the opposing attorney may object to any new opinions expressed at the trial on the grounds that you did not reveal them during the deposition.

Answer questions with *yes* or *no*, not with *un-huh* or a nod of the head. The court reporter will have trouble taking down your response. Do not repeat questions or start sentences with *a....* or *um....* These responses will prove embarrassing when read back in court. Take turns speaking with the attorneys. The court reporter can only record one person at a time.

Yes or no. In some instances, you can be required to give a simple *yes* or *no* answer, but you have a right to explain your one-word reply.

Be very careful in estimating time, speed and distance. Most people cannot do so accurately. The opposing attorney may be trying to trip you up.

Refer to documents by name or number. This makes you look professional. Do not just point.

When relaying conversations, indicate whether you are paraphrasing or quoting word for word.

Here are some expressions you should not use: *honestly, in all candor, to tell the truth,* and *I am doing the best I can.* Do not use *always* or *never.* The opposing attorney will jump on adjectives and superlatives.

Avoid obscenities, racial slurs and other inappropriate language. Remember, every word is being recorded. Snide and contentious remarks may take on a meaning you did not intend, when transcribed. Attempts at humor will not be appreciated by those who are paying for your time.

If at any time during the deposition you become confused, ask for a break to go to the bathroom. Then confer with your client-attorney. Of course, the opposing attorney may note the consultation on the record when you return.

If you become tired, ask for a break. Many witnesses have given inaccurate testimony because they lost the ability to concentrate on the question.

You versus the opposing attorney. Remember that lawyers are professionals. They work with words for a living. Each opposing attorney has his or her own technique and approach, but here are some standard types to watch for:

● **The pal** is an examiner who is disarmingly friendly. Remember, depositions are an adversary proceeding. Anyone trying to be your pal is sneaking up on you.

- **The freight train** moves at a fast pace. He or she is trying to make you talk before you think.

- **The butterfly** jumps from subject to subject unpredictably rather than pursuing one line of questioning at a time. He or she is trying to confuse you, hoping you will give conflicting testimony.

- **The cunning linguist** subtly twists your words (usually when you appear exhausted) to ask a trick question so that you give an answer that will be damaging when you hear it read at trial.

- **The timebomb** saves the difficult questions for the end of the deposition when you are tired.

Q: *Did you discuss this case with your attorney?*
  The opposing attorney is trying to get you to agree your deposition testimony is rehearsed.
A: *Yes, of course. We reviewed the facts of the case over breakfast.*

Do not argue or become angry with the opposing attorney. If you feel yourself getting mad, ask for a break. Sarcasm, belligerence and loss of composure may lead to careless testimony and certainly make an adverse impression. Do not undermine your credibility and ability to persuade. Do not tempt the opposing attorney to taunt you in court hoping you will blurt out a damaging or poorly conceived answer.

Q: *What are you going to testify to at trial?*
A: *That depends upon what I am asked. I will not volunteer any information. I will only answer questions.*

Q: *What is (the opposing witness's) reputation in your field?*
  This is a trick. He or she wants you to say the other expert is outstanding.
A: *Counselor, it is not up to me to qualify your witness.*

Your client-attorney may or may not ask a few clarifying questions at the end of the deposition. He or she is only there to protect you; to defend you from harassment and protest improper lines of questioning by making objections or instructing you not to answer. Your client-attorney is not there to interrogate you.

The opposing attorney may neglect to ask you about your qualifications. This is a trick. If for some reason you are unable to appear at the trial, your deposition can be read to the jury only if you have been *qualified*. Your background must be brought out to lay a foundation for your opinion. If the opposing attorney neglects to ask you about your qualifications, your client-attorney should examine you or enter your curriculum vita into evidence. It will then be attached to the deposition as an exhibit.

Video is being used increasingly in depositions, especially when it is known the expert will not be available for trial. The video camera is not just another recording device. Jurors are accustomed to professional talent on their television screens. You must be aware of the camera and be mediagenic. If you think you may be videotaped, take a course. Many authors take them to learn how to act on talk shows.

Attending your opposing expert's deposition. If your client-attorney is not extremely knowledgeable in the subject, he or she should have you attend the depositions of the other side's key witnesses. You will be able to see problems and suggest lines of questioning. If you do not attend the deposition, questions may go unanswered, making trial preparation more difficult.

Search for everything the opposing expert has ever written or done on this subject. If the opposing expert has testified previously in a related matter, obtain and study the transcript.

Have the expert identify and categorize each item in his or her file. Your client-attorney may wish to have each piece marked as deposition exhibits.

The opposing expert should be asked all the questions mentioned in *investigating the opposing witness* in Chapter Five, along with the following:

1. Has the expert prepared any reports that are not in the file?

2. If the expert has not produced a written report, was this on instruction of counsel or anyone else?

3. What work has been performed on this case? When was the expert first contacted by the opposing attorney? What is the exact nature of the assignment? What does the expert charge? How many hours have been spent on reading, discussion, tests, and site visits?

4. Has the expert been assisted by anyone else and, if so, what type of work was performed? (An assistant could hold an inconsistent opinion.)

5. What additional work does the expert plan to perform on the case? What additional work would the expert like to perform if he or she had an unlimited budget?

6. What is the expert's opinion, tentative or final, on each issue involved in the case? Has the expert arrived at any other opinions not already mentioned?

7. What is the basis or foundation for each opinion? On what facts, assumptions, publications or other factors has he or she relied?

8. Is the expert aware of any opinions, facts or articles which are contrary to his or her own opinion?

Transcript. The deposition transcript will be sent to you for review and signing. Make sure the court reporter understood your technical words and did not make any transcription errors. You should read, correct and then sign the transcript in front of a notary public as soon as possible and return it.

If you made a mistake during the deposition, say so and correct it. It is far better to clarify the record immediately than to be challenged at the trial. Retain copies of your past depositions so you can always see what you said in an earlier case. Sharp opposing attorneys will dig out these transcripts to search for conflicting testimony.

Save the deposition transcripts of other experts in your field, as well. You may be able to use their words against them in the future.

Payment. The (opposing) attorney who requested the deposition is responsible for paying you and for the deposition expenses. Your client-attorney will pay for copies of the transcript. Charge your client-attorney for the time it takes you to review the transcript. See Chapter Twelve on fees for details.

Review this chapter before you attend a deposition.

Sample Deposition Instructions
From the Opposing Attorney

To The Expert Witness:

This proceeding is known as a Deposition. The person transcribing the proceedings is a Certified Shorthand Reporter, and also a Notary Public who has placed you under oath. During the course of this proceeding, I, and perhaps other of the counsel present here today, will be asking you questions pertaining to this lawsuit.

Although this proceeding is being held in an informal atmosphere, since you have been placed under oath, your testimony here today has the same force and effect and is subject to the same penalties as if you were testifying in a courtroom, before a judge. Specifically, you are subject to the penalty of perjury. Perjury is defined as willfully, and contrary to an oath administered, stating as true any material fact which one knows to be false. The penalty for perjury may be imprisonment for not less than one (1) year, nor more than fourteen (14) years. You are advised that an unqualified statement of that which you do not know to be true is equivalent to a statement of that which you know to be false.

If, at any time during the deposition, you feel that any question is ambiguous or unintelligible, or that you are unable to understand it, or you fail to hear the question for any reason whatsoever, please tell the person asking you the question. If you do not so indicate, it will be presumed that you have heard and have understood each question and that your answer to each question is based upon your complete and full understanding thereof. If, after a question has been posed to you, you have any question yourself relating to what has been inquired about, please tell the person who posed the question before you answer his question.

The reporter is only able to transcribe audible responses, so please do not nod your head, shake your head, or say ahha or haah. Further, the reporter can usually record the words of only one person speaking at a time, so please allow time for the question to be completed before you respond. You will normally be allowed to finish each and every answer before a new question is posed.

At the conclusion of this deposition, the reporter will transcribe these proceedings into a booklet form, and you will have an opportunity to read that booklet and make any changes in your testimony, as it is given here today. I will be entitled to ask you why you made such changes, and comment upon those changes before a Judge or jury trial of this action. Because of that fact, it is important that all of your answers be full, complete, and correct.

If I ask you about any conversation you have had in the past, and you are unable to recall the exact words used in the conversation, you may state that you are unable to recall those exact words, and then you may give me the gist or substance of any such conversation, to the best of your recollection. If you recall only part of a conversation, or only part of an event, you are requested to give me your best recollection of those events, or parts of conversations that you recall. If I ask you whether you have any information upon a particular subject, and you have overheard other persons conversing with each other regarding it, or have seen correspondence or documentation regarding it, please tell me that you do have such information, and indicate the source, either a conversation or documentation, or otherwise, from which you derive such knowledge. In answering, please do not be concerned with whether or not your answer is hearsay or concern yourself with any technical rules of evidence you think may preclude answering.

Our purpose here today is not to trap you, or to trick you in any manner, but simply to ascertain and discover that information about the facts concerning this lawsuit that you have within your knowledge.

At the conclusion of this deposition, the attorneys present may, by agreement, stipulate that you sign the booklet containing your testimony in the presence of any notary public, rather than the reporter who is here today, taking and transcribing this deposition. If we do so, it will be upon the expressed understanding, and your promise, that you will, upon receipt of the deposition, promptly and as expeditiously as possible, read it, correct it if you feel it is necessary, and sign it in the presence of a notary public, and return it to the office from which it was sent to you.

Do you understand everything that you have just read? (Please circle)

YES   NO

Do you have any questions pertaining to either the procedure, or what is about to transpire, insofar as this Deposition is concerned? If so, please ask them of me now.

Please indicate that you have read and understood all of the foregoing, by signing this document where indicated below.

Signature of Deponent

Exhibit #   to the Deposition of   ,
taken on   , 19   .

Some of the material in this chapter will be repeated in the next chapter on the trial. This is meant to offer full coverage of each situation and make the material easier to review before the deposition or trial.

CHAPTER ELEVEN

The Trial

In going to court, you are a new player in a game with a strict set of rules. The game is called the *adversary system of justice*.

Many people find it distasteful but the regular players, the judges and attorneys, love it. They are professionals who do this for a living and they have the home field advantage. The expert witness also has an advantage, however; no one in the courtroom knows as much about the subject as the expert.

To the expert witness, testimony is a serious effort to arrive at a fixed and incontrovertible truth. To a lawyer, the trial offers challenge and excitement. Under cross-examination, you will be attacked, your expertise questioned, and your honor impugned. Yet, at the end of the day, your client-attorney and the opposing attorney may leave the courtroom together and go out for a drink.

Basically, you will be involved in two types of cases: Civil (between two or more people or companies) and criminal (the government against a person or company).

Preparation is the most important part of presenting effective and persuasive forensic evidence in either type of case. The trial is your *final exam* and the passing grade is 100%. You may spend five days reading, reviewing and anticipating for two hours on the stand. A well-prepared attorney-expert witness team is rarely surprised.

A good expert witness will:

Know the rules. Read this book, especially the chapters on depositions, trial, A Guide to the Law and the Courts and the Federal Evidence Rules. Review the procedures for the trial and the basic rules of testifying. If you know the rules of the game, you will play it better.

Know the legal issues and the applicable law. Understand the theory of the case and the place you occupy in it. Have a clear understanding of your client-attorney's objectives. You must understand the relevancy of your testimony.

Understand legal definitions. You do not want to be trapped by a misunderstanding during cross-examination.

Re-read the entire file (every deposition, etc.) in light of what you know about the case today. Underline, take notes, and add to your *narrative* outline of the facts of the case. You want to refresh your memory on what you said and what everyone else has said so far. In complex cases, you may have to compile an index so that you can locate the material you need quickly.

Base your opinion on legally permissible grounds. Generally, all tests and facts must be entered into evidence.

Review direct examination testimony with the client-attorney. Practice your testimony in the same manner and form you will use at trial. But avoid scripting your answers or you may sound mechanical. Some jurors will be hostile or bored. They didn't volunteer, they were drafted. Some will be bored and some will be concerned with outside problems. You must gain and maintain their participation. Help them to understand the scientific aspects of your case. Show them you are a nice person. Persuade them to accept your version of what happened.

Know all the players: opposing attorneys, judge, jurors, opposing experts. Note the idiosyncrasies and pet habits of the opposing attorney. Decide which jurors to address with each part of your presentation.

Ask the client-attorney about the judge's preferences. Will he or she allow you to narrate a string of events in response to a single question or will the judge insist on short answers? At least one federal judge in Oregon requires experts to file their testimony in writing before the trial and only allows them to read from the document verbatim at the trial. Know what to expect.

Suggest and prepare exhibits to illustrate your testimony. They must be large enough to see and clear enough to understand.

Make sure you have done a thorough analysis, run all tests, etc.

Find out if the opposing attorney asks questions in an irritating manner, does a lot of finger pointing or otherwise tries to make a witness feel uncomfortable. If you were deposed by this attorney, think about how you were treated.

Discuss these mannerisms and your best counter with your client-attorney.

Anticipate cross-examination questions. Plan your answers. Go over your deposition and formulate explanations for any difficult areas. Research and write out all the facts so you can rattle off your answers quickly if asked. There may be information you want to slip into the answers to other questions. Practice the cross-exam with your attorney. Review all possible questions so you won't be caught off guard on the stand. Make sure you have credible explanations in response to all potential areas of attack. If you are not prepared for 90% or more of the questions, your client-attorney has not done a good job.

If this is a major case and there is more than one expert witness, coordinate your work with the other experts. Your testimony should be consistent and should not overlap. You do not want the opposing attorney to use you to impeach each other. Read their opinion papers and spend a good deal of time discussing the case. If you get to know the other expert's position and philosophy, you will be able to predict what he or she would say. This preparation is especially important if you are *sequestered* (kept out of the courtroom) and not allowed to hear the testimony of the other expert. Never disparage the other expert when you are on the stand.

Practice, practice, practice. Anticipate questions and practice the answers. Do not try to wing it.

Going to court. Get a good night's rest. Eat a good breakfast. This is one day it is OK not to stick to your diet. Do not drink alcohol for 24 hours prior to the trial. If you are on medication, tell your client-attorney. You want to be sharp.

Dress to be credible. Project confidence. Look the part and wear whatever you wear on the job. For men, this normally means a suit or conservative jacket and tie. Women should wear a conservative dress or suit, no pants suits. Be neat. People perceive a sloppy dresser as a person who is also careless in details of testimony. You want to give the impression that you are a serious, quiet, careful individual.

Just as clothes make an impression, so do bearing, gestures and tone of voice. Convey a sense of authority with good posture. Restrain gestures. Look like an expert.

Take only your file folder with curriculum vita, fee schedule, narrative, time sheets, bills, reports, and opinion backup documents. Take all facts and data upon which you relied in forming your opinion, but only what you want the other side to have. Anything in your file is discoverable. Show the file to your attorney in the meeting prior to your testimony. He or she will want to filter out all non-discoverable (privileged) information.

Give yourself plenty of time to find a parking place and get to the courtroom. Sit in the spectator section of the courtroom unless witnesses have been sequestered (kept out of the courtroom except when testifying).

Watch the judge, jury and opposing attorneys and keep score cards on each. Whenever you see any of them writing, note the subject of the testimony at the time. A later check of your notes will reveal the issue they found of interest. Later, you may address these matters in your testimony. You will know the *players* better and this information may provide clues about the outcome of the case.

Pay attention and show respect. Do not read, chew gum, talk or sleep in the courtroom. Jurors feel this is serious business and could be offended. Do not react favorably or unfavorably to testimony. Jurors may take note of your reactions.

Unless this is a highly technical case where you must continually advise the client-attorney, it is best to stay away from the other people in the trial. Do not pass notes to your client-attorney in court. You do not want to appear to be partial to the client in the eyes of the jury.

Do not discuss the case in hallways, bathrooms or anywhere you might be overheard. You could be overheard by a juror or give your case away to the opposition.

Do not take family or friends to court to *watch the fun.* Their presence may distract you and cause you to give less than the 100% performance you are being paid for.

Direct examination. The direct examination is the unfolding of a story told from your side's point of view — and you have an assigned role. Understand the point of your appearance and the part of the overall story you are supposed to supply. You should never have a bad direct examination because you have control over it and a lot of time to prepare for it.

Most attorneys prefer that notes not be taken to the stand. But in some cases it is not unreasonable for you to refer to notes in order to be accurate. If your case deals with many figures, for example, you may wish to have these facts with you. Clear these notes with your client-attorney. Remember, the opposing attorney has a right to see any notes you testify from.

Walk to the witness stand with even steps. Carry the folder in your left hand so you won't fumble when raising the right hand to take the oath. It is difficult to regain your composure after dropping the folder contents on the floor. Be confident. Stand upright when taking the oath. Hold your right arm up high with the fingers straight, look the administering officer straight in the eye and say *I do* in a clear voice.

If you have written books on the subject, stack them where the jury can see them.

Sit down in the witness chair confidently. Do not dive into it and do not lean back. Lean forward slightly, keep your hands on the arm rests and look attentive.

Use hand gestures sparingly and only for emphasis. The court reporter can only record words. Count on your fingers to emphasize major points.

First the expert witness must be *accepted* by the judge as an expert in the precise field involved. The technical witness is qualified through skill, training, knowledge or experience. The witness must be an expert, not just someone with experience. You are there to help the jury understand how or why the event happened. Qualifications must be proven to the judge so talk to the judge.

The judge will also determine if an expert is necessary. Cases have been reversed for not allowing an expert to testify, but so far none have been reversed for allowing expert testimony.

Presentation during examination and cross-examination is made to the jury. Explain to them. Do not talk down to the jury. Be frank and open, as if you were a friend or neighbor. Be sincere, use simple terms. Make eye contact; watch the jurors, see what they think. Do they understand? Are they confused or nodding? If they are not nodding, rephrase and explain again.

Your client-attorney will present your testimony in three phases. He or she will:

1. **Offer your qualifications** as an expert to the judge. Your client-attorney will ask you questions about the more relevant portions of your curriculum vita. Present your accomplishments modestly and with a minimum of embellishment. You want to impress the jury, not alienate them. Some of these average people may have an anti-intellectual bias. Review your own CV and be precise about figures and dates. The way you answer these initial questions is important as the jury will be getting their first impression of you.

The opposing attorney may offer to *stipulate* your qualifications. This means he or she accepts that you are qualified and there is no need to take up court time reviewing your past. In a jury trial, this is a trap. Review of your qualifications is essential to prepare the judge and jury for complete acceptance of your testimony.

The judge is usually anxious to get through the qualification issue and hear what you have to say. He or she probably has a copy of your CV and knows who you are.

2. **Lay the foundation** for your opinions (tests, investigations, facts, etc.) The expert may base his opinion on three sources (Federal Rules of Evidence #703):

a. Acts observed first hand

b. Evidence presented at trial

c. Data examined outside the court and prepared by a third party (hearsay). The evidence (report) must be of a type reasonably relied upon by experts in the particular field in forming opinions or inferences.

3. **Ask for your opinion.** You will explain what is the general practice in the industry, what caused the accident, etc.

The line of questioning under direct examination proceeds in steps.

(after a line of questioning)
Q: *And based on that, do you have an opinion as to what caused the accident?*
A: *Yes, I do.*
Q: *And what is that opinion?*
A: (Whereupon you state your findings.)

Your client-attorney is not allowed to use leading questions or to question you in areas outside your stated expertise. Therefore, the questions will tend to be short, specific and to build on one-another.

Your attorney will ask broad questions (*explain lift* in an aviation case) to give you an opportunity to teach. Use the drawing board, or other demonstrative evidence, and elaborate. Present your case point-by-point.

Organization of a trial. The plaintiff (or prosecution) presents its side first. Then the defendant presents its side. You will testify during the presentation made by your side. Expert witnesses usually follow lay (fact) witnesses. For scheduling purposes, some witnesses may be taken out of turn but doing so could interrupt the flow of the presentation and confuse the jury. Also see the *A Guide to the Law and the Courts* in Chapter 18.

The judge decides questions of *law* and the admissibility of evidence (what the jury may see or hear). The jury decides questions of *fact,* how much weight to give the evidence (whether to believe you.) Therefore, evidence may be allowed by the judge but held to be weak by the jury. Talk to the decision-makers.

You must know the law governing your field of expertise, but do not offer legal opinions in the course of your testimony. Interpretations of the law are up to your client-attorney and the judge.

Juries normally consist of six, eight or twelve people depending upon the court. There will also probably be two alternate jurors who will sit through the entire trial in case one of the regular jurors should become incapacitated. The alternates will not be involved in the deliberations at the end of the trial.

In a *court trial* and in suits against the U.S. Government, there is no jury. The judge decides both law and fact. For clarity, we are going to assume there is a jury.

The lawyer's job is to ask questions. He or she is the advocate. The witness' job is to answer questions. He or she is more an educator than an advocate. The expert takes an oath to tell the truth, the whole truth and nothing but the truth. The attorney does not.

The expert's role is not to find the truth, or to find the facts, or to find who is right and who is wrong. That is up to the jury.

Address the judge as *Your Honor.* Address the attorneys by title and last name. For example, *Ms. Jones.*

On the stand. Direct *answers* to the attorney and *explanations* to the jury. If your answer is going to be over three sentences, turn to the jury. Limit your answers to ten sentences or the jury will turn off.

Explain your answers clearly so that the least intelligent juror will be sure to understand what you are saying. If you must use technical jargon, be sure to explain each term as you use it. You want to impress the jury but you also want them to understand and you do not want to talk down to them.

Powerful language will make you appear more knowledgeable. Say *yes*, not *I suppose so*. Use *93 minutes* not *around an hour and a half*. Say *60 miles per hour*, not *about as fast as a car*. Generalities will make you appear imprecise and/or unsure.

Do not use words you don't use everyday. Using big impressive words may confuse the lawyers while the judge and the jury won't trust you. There are a lot of new terms in the legal game and some have peculiar meanings. Make sure you understand them before you use them.

Be a gentle, knowledgeable educator. Avoid buzzwords. Use analogies (*victor airways are highways in the sky*). Be lively and interesting. Practice on a friend. Be direct—don't weasel. Avoid monotone: change the volume, pitch and tone of your voice from time to time. Be confident and self-assured, but not arrogant. Do not memorize testimony; sound natural and unrehearsed. Take a dose of modesty, good humor and patience with you to the stand.

Some jurisdictions allow the jurors to take notes. If they are writing furiously, slow down.

If you lean slightly against your client-attorney when answering, the jurors will be more likely to believe you are fair, reasonable and competent.

Q: *Would you say...?*
A: *No, but I would say...*

Be careful about taking sides. Do not offer to say whatever your client-attorney wants. Next time, you could find him on the other side and he will ask you about the incident to show you are a *hired gun.*

Your presentation to your client-attorney or to the jury is like a speech. Define your purpose and consider what message you want to leave. Get organized. Be concise. Make every word count. Do not use unnecessarily long explanations or repeat yourself.

There will be times when you will be more effective in getting your point across by using a single dramatic explanation in your testimony to highlight a point you want the jury to remember. Compare the following answers:

Q: *Do you have an opinion as to whether a reasonably prudent pilot would have attempted a takeoff with this damaged aircraft under those conditions?*
A: *Yes, I do.*
Q: *And what is that opinion?*
A: *I do not think he would have.*
Now consider the same line of questioning with this answer:

A: *I would not have attempted a takeoff under those conditions unless there was a tidal wave coming over the hill.*

Be very careful in estimating time, speed and distance. Since many people cannot estimate them accurately, the opposing attorney may try to trip you up. Think about the facts beforehand so you can be accurate. If you are estimating, say so.

Refer to exhibits by number. This approach makes you look more polished and credible and helps the court recorder make a clear written transcript of your testimony; very important if either side appeals the decision.

Be enthusiastic about your data but do not be an advocate for your client.

The client-attorney is the captain of the team. You are part of the legal system support team. You should support his or her line as long as it is ethically feasible. Do not take over the lead. He or she is juggling the order of the presentation, timing, which witnesses to call and in what order and much more. If you try to do something your way, you could botch the case.

If you answer a question incorrectly, correct yourself as soon as possible.

If your client-attorney asks you the same question twice, consider it a signal that your last answer was not what he or she wanted or was not clear enough. When a question is repeated, there is a inclination to start with *As I said...* or to simply repeat the answer. Don't. Just answer the question differently. Your client-attorney wants you to rephrase it and elaborate on it.

There will be times when it appears that your client-attorney has forgotten to bring out essential facts. You can remind him or her by inserting some key words into the answer for another question. He or she may have changed strategy or may simply have forgotten. Your reminder cannot hurt.

You may not mention insurance or that a woman has remarried. The revelation of either one may lead to a costly mistrial.

Unlike laymen, experts may express opinions relative to matters not observed. Experts may use hearsay evidence if inherently reliable and customarily relied upon by experts in forming their opinion; e.g., a doctor may rely on lab tests.

Be prepared to deal with inconsistencies. Don't contradict other technical witnesses on your side.

The general impression you leave with the jury is more important than answering every question perfectly. Juries often go with the expert they like the best; the one they find the most believable. Do not worry about the things you didn't say. Just make sure the things you did say were well said.

Unless the judge *sequesters* the witnesses (banishes them from the courtroom), sit through as much of the trial as possible. Listen to the other witnesses. Get to know the players. Sit in back of the courtroom, do not sit with client's people. You must appear objective.

Demonstrative evidence. Use demonstrative evidence such as models and charts to help the jury visualize the problem.

Keep your drawings and models covered until ready for presentation. Build the jury's curiosity, do not distract them during earlier testimony. See Chapter Nine on demonstrative evidence.

Try to leave your charts and other demonstrative evidence uncovered when the other side is presenting its case or cross-examining. Leave important pieces of evidence in view so they will make a continuing impression on the jury.

Opposing expert. Your opposing expert will be telling the same story, but his or her version has a different ending.

Know what the opposing expert said. Try to be there during his or her trial testimony. Some experts write furiously on a pad while the opposing expert testifies. The object is to make him or her more careful as well as curious about the notes being taken.

Know your opposing expert witness. Find everything he or she has ever published. Investigate his or her background. Find what his or her teachers have published. He or she might not contradict them. If the expert has testified before, contact the lawyers involved and get copies of the depositions and testimony transcripts. Evaluate responses and search for contradictions. Help your client-attorney to discredit or limit testimony of the opposing witness.

Make a few telephone calls to check the opposing expert's background. Verify each item on his or her curriculum vita. Your client-attorney will have an opportunity to attack the expert's credibility, and what you find could be very useful.

Be restrained in your greeting of the opposing expert, even if you know him or her well. A jury member might see your exchange and your credibility could be damaged. Of course, you should not discuss the case with the opposing expert.

Sequestration. While the court is an open proceeding, some judges feel trials move faster and that testimony is less tainted if all witnesses are *sequestered*. It is frustrating for the expert witness to wait in a room or hallway not knowing when he or she will be called or what is going on. It is a handicap to enter a courtroom without knowing the identity and placement of all the players. It is even more difficult when the opposing attorney recounts prior testimony for your evaluation and you do not know if his or her phrasing is accurate.

If the judge orders sequestration, your client-attorney should object, saying that he or she needs you to listen and advise because your technical help is important to the case. It is worth a try.

If you are excluded from the courtroom, visit another trial in the same building to get a feel for the layout and atmosphere. If you do leave the area, make sure your client-attorney knows where to find you.

In very important cases, you may request daily transcripts of the testimony so that you will not be more than a couple of days behind.

Cross-examination. The cross-examination is a challenge. It provides you with an additional opportunity to explain what happened, as well as to influence the jury.

The opposing attorney has three missions during cross-examination:

1. **To discredit you.** He or she will attack your conduct and character. The cross-examiner will try to show you have little or no theoretical, educational or practical experience or knowledge of the *particular* problem. This experience can be devastating to first-time expert witnesses who have spent a lifetime building a reputation and who are not used to having their integrity or word questioned. You may counter by reciting your credentials from your CV. The cross-examiner will try to show inconsistencies in statements you

have made. He or she has reviewed everything you have ever written.

2. To discredit the foundations for your opinions. The opposing attorney will question whether you have run enough tests, examined enough facts, etc. to be able to form a valid opinion. For example: *How can you be sure if you have not visited the scene of the accident?* He or she will try to discredit some of your tests and other evidence and may try to have some or all of your testimony eliminated because you failed to run the right tests.

Q: *Did you do AB&C?*
He wants to make you look as though you did not do your homework.
A: *Of course not. Such a test would not prove anything here.*
He probably will not dare to ask you to explain.

3. To discredit your conclusions (testimony). The opposing attorney may try to show you are confused and therefore could be wrong. He will have to know a lot about the subject to challenge you here. But be careful; he may.

The opposing attorney will attack you in two ways. First he or she will attack you as a witness with the hope of disqualifying you. Then he or she will attack your evidence. He or she wants to appear to be skillful, knowledgeable and fair while making you look evasive, partial and confused: a fool or a liar.

Q: *Are you being paid to testify?*
A: *No sir, I am not being paid to testify. I am being paid for my time, my testimony is my own. My fee was agreed upon in advance and does not depend upon the outcome of the case, I am being paid no matter who wins.*

You are not being paid for your opinion. You are being paid to study the case and form an opinion (come to a conclusion.) You are charging the client your normal hourly rate. If you were not here, you would be working somewhere else. Do not be embarrassed to say how much you charge. The higher the amount, the more you are worth. It is the person who is reluctant to tell the jury how much he or she is being paid who can be corrupted by a lot of money.

Of course, you may always answer the question your way:
A: *My company bills $140. per hour.*

Q: *Do you often testify as an expert witness?*
A: *Yes.*
Q: *Then you are a professional expert, a hired gun?*
A: *I would like to think that I am being consulted frequently because of my professional competence and reputation.*

Your client-attorney may bring up the compensation question more gently during the direct examination. This is a tactic to defuse the question, to take this offensive play away from the opposing attorney.

This same tactic may be used whenever you think the opposing side will bring up an uncomfortable topic. For example, if you made a statement in your deposition which you wish to alter now, your client-attorney may bring it up and ask you to explain the reason for the change.

When the opposing attorney attacks your credibility, keep calm. His or her actions are not unexpected. You knew what to expect. It is all part of the job, and the best way for the expert to survive is to play the game. The jury is likely to be favorably impressed if you stay cool under pressure.

Do not argue with the opposing attorney and do not defend yourself. Try not to become flustered, stubborn, or recalcitrant; to do so is to concede your point. Use the opportunity to further persuade the jury. Turn to the jury and give a whole new explanation. The opposing attorney will probably be afraid to ask too many questions if he finds he is only opening the door for you. You do not win by slaying your opposing witness, you win when the jury accepts your version of the problem.

Never look at your client-attorney while you are being cross-examined. Everyone will think you are waiting for a signal.

Trial techniques vary. Professional opponents can be a joy to work with. They let you answer and do your job. They deserve straight answers. On the other hand, if the opposing attorney is nasty, or disruptive, it is OK to slip in a zinger now and then. Just make sure the judge and jury are disgusted with the opposing attorney's conduct first. Some of those *I–wish–I'd–said–that* answers are noted in this chapter.

Refuse to be browbeaten. Cross-examinations are limited to matters covered in the examination, but witness credibility may be attacked at any time. Calmly point out where the opposing attorney is wrong. The jury recognizes when an attorney is out of line. Think of yourself as being on a television talk show where the host is giving you a hard time.

Some expert witnesses prefer to have a competent attorney on the other side. It is hard to give an intelligent answer to a stupid question.

Remember, the opposing attorneys are good at what they do. They cross-examine witnesses for a living. But, as good as they are, they do not know as much about your subject as you do.

Q: *Have you ever been accused of anything?*
A: *Yes sir, I have been accused of just about everything.*

Juries enjoy accidental humor but are offended by deliberate humor—especially from women. To them, this is serious business. Jurors believe they have an important job.

Follow these three basic rules during cross-examination:

1. **Listen to the question and pause before answering it.** The pause permits you to formulate your answer and allows your client-attorney to object to the question if it is improper.

If your client-attorney objects, stop talking and wait for the judge to rule. You will be told to answer the question or you will be given a new question.

Analyze the question. It may be *vague and ambiguous.* Do not guess. Make sure you understand all the terms used. Do not hesitate to have the question reworded. If you do not express a lack of understanding, it will be presumed that you understand the question and that your answer is a full and complete response to it.

If you think the opposing attorney is trying to be tricky, ask him or her to rephrase the question so that the meaning will be clearer.

When a (compound) question has many parts, ask to have it rephrased in single elements. Be alert for questions containing the words *or* or *and.*

The opposing attorney may ask you a question which does not call for new facts. The question is considered *argumentative* if he or she is seeking an explanation of a previous answer.

Watch for questions that inaccurately summarize prior testimony or assume facts that are untrue. Do not accept this characterization of data, assumptions or descriptions of events. Listen carefully and point out each and every inaccurate statement in the summarization.

Assumptions may only be made on facts which are in evidence. *Foundation* must exist or your answer will admit the assumed fact.

2. **Look directly at the attorney** asking the question. People equate eye contact with sincerity. They assume that those who can't look you in the eye must be hiding something.

Give a responsive answer but do not volunteer additional information. Do not give him or her an opening to another line of questioning. Remember, the longer the answer, the more you are liable to be giving away.

Answer questions with *yes* or *no*, not *un-huh* or with a nod of the head. The court recorder will have trouble taking down your response. Take turns speaking. The court recorder can only record one person at a time.

Here are some expressions you should not use: *honestly, in all candor, to tell the truth,* and *I am doing the best I can.* Do not use *always* or *never.* The opposing attorney will jump on adjectives and superlatives.

3. **Tell the complete truth.** It is better to say *I do not know* or *I do not remember* than to make a guess.

Q: *Would you swear that is what happened in your tests?*
A: *I was sworn to tell the truth when I took the stand.*

Be fair and frank. Do not be too anxious to please or too eager to fight. Do not argue or become angry with the opposing attorney. An angry witness is not listening to the questions and is prone to volunteer unasked–for information. This is precisely what the opposing attorney is hoping for. It is always better to smile and proceed. Sarcasm, belligerence and loss of composure may lead to careless testimony and they certainly make an adverse impression. Do not undermine your credibility and ability to persuade.

Respond respectfully. Accept counsel's aggression graciously. He or she has a right to question you. If you respond with smart talk or an evasive answer, he or she may jump down your throat or the judge may correct you. (Be wary of a nice opposing attorney, too—he or she may be sneaking up on you.)

If the opposing attorney becomes abusive, you should become more of a gentlemen (or lady). One way to show your concern without revealing your anger is to say *Counsel, your attitude is so offensive, I could not concentrate on the question.*

Q: When did you form your opinion on the case?
  (See the discussion in Chapter Four on opinion forming.)

When relaying conversations, indicate whether you are paraphrasing or quoting verbatim.

Q: Do you enjoy being an expert witness?
A: I enjoy seeing justice being done.

Your credibility as an expert witness is based on five factors:

1. Your qualifications

2. The accuracy and thoroughness of your investigation and personal observations

3. The accuracy of the hypothetical question or other information supplied to you on cross-examination

4. The validity of your conclusions

5. Your appearance, demeanor and attitude on and off the stand.

Avoid obscenities, racial slurs and other inappropriate language. Remember, every word is being listened to by the jury and recorded by the court recorder.

Leading questions are those containing the answer, to which you are only asked to agree. They are *leading* because you have been given the answer. Your client-attorney may not be allowed to use leading questions during your direct or re-direct examination. However, the opposing attorney is permitted to use leading questions during cross-examination and re-cross. If any part of the question is not correct, you may say that you cannot *entirely* agree.

Hypothetical questions combine facts and circumstances and ask you to conjecture an opinion. Hypothetical questions must not be misleading or unfair but they are almost always a sign of a mine field. *Suppose this were the case....* or, *Assuming this and that and this, what would you expect a rational person in this area to do?* Keep your eyes open and tread carefully.

Hypothetical questions asking you to assume facts must:

1. Be supported by the evidence (facts which have been admitted into evidence by one side or the other)

2. Be factually consistent

3. Contain enough facts to draw a probable conclusion.

A: *yes, but...*

A: *That is a great hypothetical question but it does not apply to this situation. So, my hypothetical answer to your hypothetical question has to be...*

The plaintiff is advancing one set of facts and their expert draws a conclusion. The defendant advances another set of facts and their expert draws a different conclusion. The jury has to decide which set of facts to believe.

Treat the opposing attorney the same way you did your client-attorney during direct examination. You are a professional, you have analyzed the facts, you are there to communicate information to the jury. Know what you said in your deposition and give the same answers, using the same words.

Do not say *That is all that happened.* Say *That is all I remember happening.* Something may trigger additional thoughts later.

Answers on cross-examination should be limited to *yes* and *no* if possible. Do not say *I think* or *I believe.* It is OK not to know minute details such as exact dates. It is OK to say *I do not remember.* Do not volunteer information or open doors for the opposing attorney to ask more questions.

If the line of inquiry strays from your field, do not stretch your credibility by pretending to know the answer. For example, if you are an expert in parachutes and you are asked if the materials and construction are the same on spinnakers, it is OK to say: *I do not know. I am not a nautical expert. If you can describe the manufacture of spinnakers, perhaps I can compare the materials and construction.* You can always say: *That requires further investigation.* Arrogant people make poor expert witnesses. Be humble.

If the question deals with the subject of your expertise and you do not know, you can always say *I was not asked to research that.*

Yes or No. You can be required to give a simple yes or no answer if the question is proper, but you have a right to explain your one-word answer.

Attorney: *Please answer with a yes or no.*
Expert: *I can't answer with a yes or no without leaving a false impression with the jury.*
Then if the judge instructs you to answer yes or no, the jury will know there is something missing. If you answer *well...no,* the opposing attorney probably will not pursue the line of questioning.

If the opposing attorney is persistent and you repeat that you wish to explain why you cannot answer with a *yes* or *no,* your client-attorney may object on the grounds that you are being harassed.

If the judge tells you to answer *yes* or *no,* it is up to your client-attorney to give you a chance to explain on re-direct.

One very effective technique for answering questions is to rephrase the question, adding an explanation so that your answer is very clear to the jury. Answer the questions as though you were being interviewed on a television talk show.

If the opposing attorney asks you the same question twice, just say you have already answered it.

The long question.
A: *The question is complex, would you mind breaking it up?*
or,

A: *Your question was so long, I got lost.*
or,
A: *I am afraid my answer is going to have to be as convoluted as your question. Why don't we take the elements one at a time?*

Do not ask the judge for advice. If the question is improper, it is up to your client-attorney to object.

If your client-attorney objects to a question as being *without foundation, misleading or improper,* take it as a signal that the question is tricky or important. Ask to have the question rephrased.

It is OK to admit you were wrong. If you do not know a fact or circumstance, do not offer to look it up. The opposing attorney will want to know where you plan to look it up, allowing him or her to subpoena records he or she may not have known existed.

Q: *Isn't this possible?*
A: *No sir, it is not possible. Not under the facts of this case.*

Avoid mannerisms, they make you look nervous and the jury will think you are not telling the truth.

Marking exhibits. If you are asked to mark a map, chart or model, make sure you fully understand it. If you are asked to pinpoint something on a map, cover yourself by saying you are not familiar with this particular map (of course, you are familiar with the *area* covered by the map). Then draw a large circle instead of a dot.

Learned treatises. Expert witnesses may not quote passages from someone else's book. They may, however, base their opinions on standard authoritative texts. If you referred to or considered a passage from a book, you can be cross-examined on the entire text. Opposing attorneys are allowed to quote passages from a book to try to impeach you as a witness. Know your field and be prepared to argue for your stand if you disagree with a learned treatise. See Federal Rules of Evidence 803 (18).

Q: *Do you agree with this book?*
A: *That book is useful but not authoritative. I read this book and all other books and based on my accumulated knowledge, my opinion is....*

Quoting your book or deposition. The most effective manner of impeaching a witness is to find a passage in his or her book or prior testimony which reaches an opposite conclusion to the one professed in court. The opposing attorney will research everything you have ever written and said.

(Opposing attorney reads passage from your book)
Q: *Did you write that?*
A: *Yes, if that was a literal reading of my book.*
Q: *Do you agree with it?*
A: *May I see the page you are reading from?*

If confronted with a passage read out of one of your books, magazine articles or past deposition transcripts, always ask to see the entire document before answering. Once you read the page, your memory will be refreshed, the passage will be *in context* and a good answer will almost always become clear to you.

But what if the conclusion in your book is different from the one you are proposing today?

Expert: *Counselor, will you please turn to the reverse of the title page in that book? It should be about page five.*
Attorney: *OK, I have it.*
Expert: *Please read the copyright date on that page.*
Attorney: *1978*
Expert: *There have been a lot of changes since 1978 and one is the current thought on that subject. Books can only reflect thought up to the day they are printed.*

If you are questioned on any part of a document on direct examination, you may be cross-examined on anything else in it. For this reason, your client-attorney may be reluctant to question you about many documents.

Q: *But didn't you publish this book yourself?*
(He or she is trying to make your book appear to be worthless because it was vanity published. That is, no reputable publisher thought enough of your manuscript to invest in it.)
A: *Yes. I publish my own books for three reasons: To keep control of the content, to get to press much faster and to make more money.*
(You can expand on each area.)

Q: *Why didn't you bring these records with you today?*
A: *Because there isn't any information in those records which is inconsistent with my testimony. I didn't need them.*

Q: *How much time do you spend in the practice of your profession as opposed to testifying?*

Remember, you are not a professional expert witness. You are a professional, working today as an expert witness. See Chapter Seven on maintaining competence.

Q: *Is all your time spent consulting?*
(What if you *are* a full-time expert witness?)
A: *Yes, I am a specialist.*

Q: *Do you always testify for the plaintiff (or defendant)?*
A: *I have a fairly even balance of cases,* or,
A: *40% of my* billings *are for the defense.*
Check your records. 40% of your billings could come from 10% of your cases.
or,
A: *Quite often, by the time the defendant hears he is being sued, I have already been hired by the plaintiff.*
or,
A: *Most of my cases have not even gone to trial because I have recommended to my defendant-client that he pay or to my plaintiff-client that he drop the case.*
or,

A: *While I have* testified *slightly more for the plaintiff, I have an even balance of cases overall. Most of my cases do not go as far as court.*
Q: *Would you agree with the statement if the student fails to learn, the instructor has failed to teach?*
A: *Some people learn and still do it their own way.*

Q: *Are (structural engineering) experts 100% correct?*
A: *I do not understand the logic of your question.*
Q: *Well, have you ever been wrong?*
A: *Of course..*

Q: *Wouldn't it be fair to say...*
You might feel it is somewhat fair to say it and you do want to be fair so you may be tempted to agree. Do not agree and explain your reason.

Some experts like to say *no* if any part of the question is wrong. Then the opposing attorney must decide if he wants to continue pursuing this line of questioning.

Q: *Do you want the jury to understand that...*
Listen closely to this one. Make it clear what you want the jury to understand.

Q: *Do you* really *believe that position?*
(You may wish to go on the offensive; to take advantage of the opening)
A: *I am glad you asked me that question. Ever since I first heard of this case and discovered what the defendant did to the plaintiff I have felt frustrated and completely disgusted.*

Q: *Don't you think a warning label would have made a difference?*
A: *No sir, warning labels have not stopped people from smoking.*

Q: *Did you discuss your testimony with counsel?*
A: *Of course. I gave him an objective description of where the case stood and he told me some of the questions I could expect to be asked. He also told me to come in here and tell the truth.*

Q: *Have you discussed this case with the opposing expert?*
A: *We are members of the same professional organizations and attend the same meetings. It is difficult to avoid meeting him, talking to him and even working with him. The subject came up; I asked him a few questions to learn more about the case but I did not volunteer any information.*

Watch for this standard cross-examination trick: After your brief answer, opposing counsel pauses and gazes at you expectantly. You feel an overwhelming pressure to say something more. Stop. If the attorney wants more, let him ask for it.

Beware of the opposing attorney who acts dumb. He or she may be trying to convince the jury this is such a complicated area, the client could not possibly have understood what he or she was getting into.

Q: *Skydiving is a very complex subject and I am having difficulty understanding it. What do I have to do to comprehend what happened?*
A: *You could do what your client did: Take the First (parachute) Jump Course.*

Q: *Doctor, what do I have to do to get you to answer the question so that I can understand what you are saying?*
A: *You could start with four years of medical school.*

All of these answers have been used. Some are guaranteed to get the expert into trouble unless the opposing attorney is badgering him.

Q: *Is skydiving dangerous?*
A: *It wouldn't be much fun if it weren't.*

Q: *Have you ever worked for this law firm in the past?*
(He or she is trying to show you are a hired gun.)
A: *Yes, Humpty, Dumpty and Gander is one of the major aviation (more specifically parachuting) law firms, and I am one of the major technical experts for parachutes so our paths often cross. In fact, I am probably the only parachute expert they know.*

It may help to study the cases you have worked on for the firm to see how you were initially contacted. You may find good reasons for working so many cases for the same firm. One might be that you were first contacted by other firms and referred to your client-attorney. For example:

My work for Humpty, Dumpty and Gander

as of September 20, 1988

Chicken v. Fox: First contacted by John Moore of Moore and Moore. He passed me on to H,D & G.

Cat v. Mouse: Contacted by Peter Levin, President of General Mouse. He recommended me to H,D & G.

Smith v. Jones: Larry Knight called me on January 11, 1987. Came to me because of work on previous cases.

Peters v. General Mouse: Recommended by General. Contacted by H,D & G on December 1, 1988. Also worked for Simple, Simon and Pie of Baltimore.

Case log

Many lawyers subscribe to the maxim *you can't win the case on direct examination but you can lose it on cross.* Be satisfied to break even on cross-examination.

Re-direct examination. The re-direct is done by your client-attorney for the purpose of clearing up confusion in the cross-examination. If you were not damaged in the cross-examination, your client attorney will *have no further questions.* If your client-attorney conducts a re-direct, the opposing attorney will get another shot at you in re-cross. Questions on re-direct are limited to the scope of the cross-examination.

Re-cross-examination. The re-cross is done by the opposing attorney. Questions are limited to the scope of the re-direct. The re-cross is usually quite short but can be crucial. Stay on your toes.

Afterwards. When you leave the witness stand, wear a confident expression and walk out of the courtroom unless your client-attorney has instructed you to stay. Do not look triumphant or relieved. Do not stop to talk to the client-attorney. You want to look impartial.

Leave the building as soon as you have approval from your client-attorney. You may have to take the stand again later to rebut some element of the opposing expert's testimony.

On the other hand, if you are still in the building, you run the risk of being called back to the stand by the opposing attorney. Also remember that as long as you are in the courthouse, you are *on stage*. It is better not to run the risk of being seen again by the jury.

During a break in testimony or when done, offer your business card to the court reporter. The kindness will be appreciated and your name will be spelled correctly.

Courtroom demeanor. Nonverbal signs may make a greater impression on the jury than your testimony. Studies show that actual words spoken may account for as little as seven percent of a message while the other 93 percent comes from nonverbal elements. In other words, how you say it is more important than what you say. The jury is weighing tone of voice, rate of speech, gestures, posture, eye contact, distance and dress. Do you look and sound like you know what you are talking about? Remember, it is not just what you know that counts, it is what the jury understands and believes you know.

Everything you do around the courthouse is significant. Your dress, speech, actions in the courtroom, meetings in the elevators, etc. Jurors are sensitive to behavior on and off the witness stand.

Do not talk to members of the jury outside the courtroom. You will see them in the halls and on the street and there will be a temptation to mention the case. Do not start a conversation. If a juror starts talking, it is better to smile and confine any chit–chat to the weather. Do not cause a mistrial.

Do not talk to the press. Be polite, offer your card but do not pour out your feelings unless you have the express permission of your client-attorney. You have been paid by your side and you have a duty and a relationship to them. They may wish to issue a written news release or to otherwise handle the press themselves. Just say that all statements will be forthcoming from your client-attorney. Remember, the case is not over until the time for appeal has lapsed.

Fatigue. Testifying for any length of time is tiring. Opposing attorneys know this and may try to tire you out so that you will lose your composure and say things that are incorrect or things that hurt you or your testimony. Symptoms of witness fatigue are tiredness, crossness, nervousness, careless answers, willingness to say anything to get off the witness stand, and anger.

Let the opposing attorney hammer away at you. If you are tired, so is the jury. They will side with you. Some attorneys strategize their case to wear down the jury. The hope is that the jury will make a quick decision just to be able to get out and go home.

If you go on the stand after lunch, the opposing attorney may try to keep you on until the end of the day with testimony to continue in the morning. That way, he or she has time to dream up some new questions and you can spend an anxious night worrying about your performance.

Subpoenas. If you are subpoenaed by a court, you must appear (if it has jurisdiction over you — generally in the same county, state or within a reasonable distance).

If you are hired by a law firm as an expert witness and you do not appear, that firm may sue you since they relied upon your testimony in building their case.

Lay witnesses (performing their civic duty) may be paid as little as $12/day plus mileage while an expert witness (providing a service) may command $800/day or more. If you are subpoenaed as a lay witness, do not give away your opinion. For example, if you are a doctor who examined the plaintiff, relay what you did in the examination but do not comment on the meaning of the tests.

If subpoenaed, you may ask your client-attorney to go to the judge to request he quash or modify the subpoena.

Specific documents and other specific tangible evidence may be ordered to court with a subpoena duces tecum. You may be ordered to bring certain items to court with you.

Before testifying in court, reread this Chapter and Chapter Ten on depositions.

CHAPTER TWELVE

How Much is Your Knowledge Worth?

Expert witnesses generally charge between $600 and $5,000 per day, depending on their type and degree of specialty.

How much you can charge depends upon the going rate as well the amount of competition. If you have developed certain special testing techniques and/or have a good reputation in the field, you can charge relatively more.

Some experts who work in small towns feel they can't charge as much as similar experts in the big city.

Some experts reduce fees for agencies such as the Legal Aid Society or do pro bono publico (for the public good or for free) work. They feel that if the attorney is willing to work without compensation, they should too.

For examples of fees in many different fields of expertise, send for *Guide to Experts' Fees* published by the National Forensic Center. The address is in the Appendix.

The amount you charge for testifying should be at least as much as your earnings from your regular work. For example, a doctor who makes $200/hour seeing patients can easily justify charging $200/hour while working on a court case. Some experts argue they should charge more because of the greater effort required and the higher level of aggravation.

According to the *Wall Street Journal*, the fees charged by lawyers have been escalating recently. In New York, some senior partners have been commanding $350 per hour. Even brand new lawyers, fresh out of law school, are charging $100 per hour. And they, presumably, have steadier work than expert witnesses.

It must be remembered that consulting is part-time work; you have overhead and you get paid only for the hours you spend on the job. Salaried people earn less per hour but they have many perks and benefits and the work is steady.

A standard fee might be $140. per hour for work done at home. This work might include investigation, research, reading depositions, telephone counselling or visits by the attorney to you. You might charge $700. per day plus expenses when hired to leave town to give depositions, do on-site investigation or testify in a trial. That means if you work at home for more than five hours in any one day, you will charge the day rate. In other words, $700. is the maximum charge for one day. Some experts disagree and publish only an hourly rate.

Do not quote a flat rate for a case. You cannot accurately estimate what it will cost. Charging by the hour is fair to both sides. You might make an exception for creating demonstrative evidence where the time and materials can be accurately estimated.

In very long cases, some experts total the hours and divide by eight to arrive at a daily rate.

Charge from portal to portal. Start the clock when you leave the house or office and stop it when you re-enter. You can justify charging for travel time because it is time you would otherwise spend productively. You can always work on the plane—and you should if you are charging the client for the time. Many litigation consultants like to use travel time to refresh their memories by reading the trial chapter of this book to get in the right frame of mind.

Some litigation consultants charge more for court room work than for waiting or travel time. Others use a simplified fee schedule like the sample which follows. Some lawyers advise the simple fee plan as they feel it is hard to justify a multi-tiered fee schedule to a jury. If you charge more for testifying than waiting to testify, it sounds as though the expert is *selling* his or her testimony—and at a premium price.

No attorney wants to go into court with the second best expert, yet some will try to get a lower rate. They should realize that the expert who acquiesces to a lower rate is usually not a professional—someone with experience testifying under pressure.

If your client-attorney asks for a lower rate for a long case, ask for a guarantee and a cancellation clause. That is, you will lower your hourly rate if you are guaranteed a minimum number of hours.

Charge the same rates for each side. You will not appear to be objective if you charge plaintiffs more or less than defendants.

Depositions. You will be paid by the opposing attorney when your deposition is taken. The scale is at your usual, published hourly rate for the deposition itself and for the time traveling to and from the deposition. If you must travel some distance, you are entitled to be compensated for hotel, meals and travel expenses. While your billable time includes travel time, it does not include the time spent preparing for the deposition. Preparation time should be billed to your client-attorney.

In some jurisdictions, such as California, you are entitled to be paid in advance based on the anticipated length of the deposition. If the examination exceeds the anticipated length, the balance of the fee is due you within five days of receipt of an itemized statement. If the fee fails to arrive prior to the deposition date, you do not have to appear. However, most experts simply attend the deposition and then send a bill for time and expenses.

If the opposing attorney does not wish to pay your regular rate, he or she may petition the court to set a reasonable fee. Any party, including the expert, may petition the judge to determine if your fees are reasonable. In some jurisdictions, there is a dollar limit on expert witness fees.

Terms. Publish your terms by sending your fee schedule to your attorney-client. Stick to the terms you have listed. An example might be:

- Billed monthly and payable net 30 days from date of invoice.
- New accounts shall be initiated with an advance payment of $500.
- All travel expenses shall be paid in advance.

- Fees for depositions shall be paid in advance based on the anticipated length of the examination. Balances due, if any, shall be paid within five days of the deposition.
- Fees for three days time shall be paid in advanced for trials or depositions outside of California, two days in California.

Advance payments. Some experts keep collecting in advance by requiring clients to maintain a minimum account balance. Credit balances are refunded at the end of the case. Do not lend money to your client-attorney. Have the air ticket sent to you. The law firm may get a better price anyway. Let them invest **their** money.

Make sure you receive the check for your air fare, estimated hotel expenses and three days of your time (probably $3,000) before you leave town for a trial. If your side loses, you may have a great deal of trouble collecting.

Q: *Does your client owe you any money?*
A: *No. My bills have been paid to date and my expenses for this trip were paid in advance. My being paid does not depend on the outcome of this case.*

Expense surcharge. Some experts add a 10% or 15% surcharge to expenses on the theory that they have paid for the hotels and air fares and anticipate a long period before they collect. It hurts when you have traveled to court, put in a good effort, finished the job, paid American Express and then have trouble collecting the reimbursement.

Attorneys can avoid these surcharges by providing the tickets for travel and signing for the hotel bill before you arrive.

On–call fees. It is virtually impossible to predict when the expert will go on the stand. You must be available when the court is ready for you. For out of town trials, you may use the same daily fee schedule for your time whether you are traveling, waiting or testifying. Your client is paying for your time no matter what you are doing. However, when you are *on–call* for a local trial, a problem arises. If you are a dentist, you may not be able to schedule your patients for *tentative* appointments. You may not be able to respond to a call to court in the middle of a root canal procedure. Dentists and many other experts have office overhead to pay whether they are working (and being paid) or not. Many expert witnesses deal with this problem by charging an *on–call* fee which is lower than their regular rate. They stay by the telephone and keep busy with other work that can be dropped at any time.

Court–hired experts and fee setting. The judge may appoint an expert to investigate, report and testify. (Federal Rules of Evidence. Rule 706). Some 30% of the experts polled by the National Forensic Center have been hired by a court at one time or another. The court set the fees in about 50% of the cases. Compensation in criminal, and some civil, cases is made by the government. In the rest of the civil cases, the court apportions the fee among the parties.

The poll also showed some 30% of the prosecutors set fees while only 9% of hiring insurance companies did.

Contingency fees. The jury is not likely to believe in an expert's objectivity if his or her fee depends on the outcome of the case. Contingency fees are prohibited in some jurisdictions. (California is one.) Some experts have been awarded contingency fees when they worked only on the pre-trial portion of the case as a consultant and did not testify at the trial. Most lawyers do not want experts to get contingency fees, however. They do not want to share.

Ordinary witnesses may be compensated as little as $12/day and 20 cents/mile. You may be subpoenaed as a fact or *percipient* (eye) witness to avoid paying your expert's fee. You will be asked what you saw in your investigation. If this happens, do not be tricked into answering opinion questions.

Your client-attorney must indemnify you against all expenses which you may be forced to pay in the case. The other side may try to depose you as a lay witness without paying you your fee, or you may have to spend several hours preparing for a deposition, or the opposition may want photocopies of your entire library as part of the discovery process. Make sure one side or the other agrees to pay you.

Who will pay? Clarify whether you will be working for the attorney or the client. You may be paid by the attorney, his or her client, an insurance company, the attorney working for a co-plaintiff or co-defendant or any party that has sufficient monetary interest in the outcome of the case. Clients may be harder to collect from. Identify who is going to pay you.

In October of 1986, Congress passed the Anti-Drug Abuse Act which defined money laundering as knowingly accepting money ($10,000. or more) from someone who earned it illegally. The object was to prevent criminals from benefiting (buying fancy cars or hiring expensive lawyers) from their crimes. This act puts attorneys, experts and others in a difficult position. In addition to a collection problem, they could be fined and jailed for accepting payment for their services. When working criminal cases, determine who will be responsible for the bill.

Do not hire subcontractors. If you need help, introduce the new (specialist) consultant or firm to the attorney and let them contract with each other. Do not become responsible for the work of others or for collecting from one firm to pay another.

Check the *Guide to Experts' Fees* and draft a fee schedule using the following example as a guide:

Michael J. Maus, R.R.

Technical investigation, consulting and testimony in rodent control cases
Fee Schedule

January 1988

For work performed in Anaheim.....$140/hour to $700/day max.

Includes investigation, research in extensive personal library (consisting of bound magazines, military specifications, video tapes, photographs, training manuals and books), counselling, trial preparation, oral and written reports.

For work performed outside of Anaheim......$700/day plus **expenses. (Billed in half days @ 350 each).

Includes investigation, counselling, oral reports, travel, depositions and court testimony. To be followed with a written report, as required.

** Expenses. Actual expenses reasonably and necessarily incurred, such as travel, subsistence and lodging, long distance telephone charges, professional support requirements, etc., are additional to the consulting fee and will be billed to the client at cost. First Class air travel (Business Class where available) is expected.

Terms:

* Billed monthly and payable net 30 days from date of invoice.
* New accounts shall be initiated with an advance payment of $500.
* All travel expenses shall be paid in advance.
* Fees for depositions shall be paid in advance based on the anticipated length of the examination. Balances due, if any, shall be paid within five days of the deposition.
* Fees for three days time shall be paid in advanced for trials outside of California, two days in California.
* Payment shall be made to Maus Associates (FEIN #95-1234567)

Mr. Maus is listed as an expert witness by the National Forensic Center, Technical Advisory Service for Attorneys, *Consultants and Consulting Organizations Directory*, and *The Lawyers Guide to Legal Consultants, Expert Witnesses, Services, Books and Products.*

Invoice #4148

<u>Cat v. Mouse, et. al.</u>

1986:

June 3: Telcon from Mr. Lyon re. case.   n/c
Telcon to Mr. Lyon .15 hours @ $110. $16.50
Telephone charges $4.50

June 10: Review folder, draft narrative and research in
own library. Telcon with Mr. Lyon 3 hours. $330.00
Call to Mr. Lyon, telephone charges $3.00

June 11: Call to Ms. Tiger. .32 hours $33.00
Telephone charges $5.50

July 10: Telcon from Mr. Lyon .45 hours $49.50

July 15: Reviewed answers to interrogatories, called Mr
Lyon. Researched files, made photocopies for Lyon .95
hours. $104.50
Call to Mr. Lyon, telephone charges $3.00
Photocopies $1.30
Postage $2.40

Subtotal $553.20
Cheque #7568 rec'd $500.00
Total due $53.20

Example of an initial invoice

CHAPTER THIRTEEN

Collections

One of the topics of greatest interest to a technical expert is getting paid. Whenever two or more experts gather, the subject of collections is often discussed. Some experts have collection problems, others get their money up–front, some feel they lose clients by being too strict about their terms and many just live with slow payments. About 25% of the expert witnesses polled by the National Forensic Center said they had collection problems.

Payment in advance. Should you demand payment in advance? Ask yourself these questions: Will the plaintiff be able to pay me if he does not recover? Will the defendant be able to pay me if he loses and has to pay a great sum to the plaintiff? Will the defendant be able to pay me if he is in jail?

The same NFC poll showed that 24% of the experts require the client-attorney to pay in advance. As justification, many of them argue that they can be more objective about the case if they have already received payment.

What you should do depends on the type of clients you are likely to have. For example, if you work for the defense in an industry covered by insurance, you will get your money when the insurance company pays the attorney. This could take several months because, while insurance companies are often good pay, they are usually slow. If you do technical analysis for the defense in drug cases, you want to get all your money up-front. Drug runners have money (can pay the bill), are desperate (will pay almost anything you ask), may not have an address (making them hard to find after the trial), are unreliable (why bother to pay after the trial), and may be part of a criminal network (making collection efforts dangerous).

The best advice is to consider the situation and contract with the attorney, not the client.

If your side loses and you are asked to lower your fee, it may look as though you are working on a contingency fee basis. Remember that contingency fees are illegal in some jurisdictions.

If the case is taken over by a new attorney, you have a right to have him or her guarantee past fees.

Bill regularly and bill more often as the work mounts. It is easier to pay a small bill than a large one. When payments are slow, some experts use certified mail/return receipt so that the client–attorney can not claim the bill or statement was not received.

Enforce collections. Suspend work until you get another advance. If it comes out in court that you have not been paid lately, the jury may think the outcome of the case is very important to you. Your objectivity may be suspect.

Many expert witnesses are charging interest for overdue bills. If you decide to do this, add a notice to your fee schedule so clients will be forewarned.

Many lawyers are not good business people and they keep poor records, so treat the work as a business. Maintain accurate billing records.

Every month, send a detailed billing like the following example. Show precisely what work has been done and what you have charged for it. Include the date, number of hours worked and a short description of the work performed. Itemize all expenses and attach photocopies of receipts. If you have a regular invoice form in your business, you may wish to use it to note *Consultation per the attached* and then include a detailed billing like the one reproduced here.

CHAPTER FOURTEEN

Investigation and Testing

To do your job properly, you must run every possible test and thoroughly research every part of your case. The opposing expert may do this and you must assume the other expert will find what you find.

If you need more information about the case, tell your client-attorney. The more investigation, analysis, research and testing you are able to do, the more credible, persuasive and comfortable you will be.

Some areas of expertise routinely require detailed testing and lengthy documentation while other areas rarely do.

Investigating the site. Visit the site of the accident and write up a report. Your trained eye may pick up relevant facts which were not disclosed in reports. Stand on all corners and become familiar with the place. Close your eyes and try to picture the scene, objects and events. Inspect the site and the equipment as soon as possible. Weather and age may alter the evidence.

Take photographs of the site and log the shots on a piece of paper. Record the date, time, item being photographed, distance and other pertinent information. Photograph any labels, placards, signs, warnings or instructions posted on the site or the evidence. After processing the photographs, label, date and sign them.

Maintain complete records of your investigation; do not rely on your memory. Details which do not seem important at first may be valuable later when new information comes to light.

If you find evidence at the site and remove it, it will require special handling. Make sure it is tagged, identified and dated.

If the opposing attorney, opposing expert or anyone else is present when you inspect the equipment or site, do not talk with them. All communications should go through your client-attorney.

Inspecting the equipment. In many types of cases, you must see the equipment in question. If the other side has it, they will be reluctant to send it to you, since it could get lost. Without it, they would not have a case. They may require your side to give them a hand receipt and a promise to give up the fight if the equipment is lost. You are usually allowed to see the gear in the office of the opposing attorney. During your inspection, he or she may remain in the room. This makes inspection and conversations with your client-attorney difficult.

During your inspection, take a lot of photographs. Once they are processed, identify, sign and date them.

Chain of custody. Establish a chain of custody for exhibits. Whenever evidence is transferred from one party to another, get hand receipts. You must be able to prove it is the *same* piece of evidence.

If you take evidence into your possession, be very careful. You could be held liable for the amount asked in the case if you lose it. The jury will not be sympathetic if evidence was lost while in your possession. Remember too, it is illegal to destroy evidence. See the forms at the end of this chapter.

Testing. The expert witness interprets scientific and technical facts and renders scientific and technical opinions based on those facts. Quite often, tests are required to establish exactly what those facts are. Your opinion will be particularly persuasive if you have tested your theories and the opposing expert has not. Tests may be conducted by an independent testing facility or you can do them yourself.

Ask yourself why the part failed. Was the failure due to *design, manufacture or usage?*

An expert is only as credible as his data. Be sure to establish the source of all questionable information and the precise procedures performed or not performed.

At the deposition, the opposing attorney will ask for a copy of your file. If he or she determines that you are relying on inaccurate or false information, this revelation may be saved for the trial.

Tests must be conducted under the same or similar conditions as those existing when the accident took place. It is necessary only that the conditions be substantially alike; they do not have to be identical.

Destructive testing may demolish the evidence, so you will have to obtain consent from both sides in the case before performing tests of this kind.

Evaluate the tests. Use recognized standards and specifications wherever possible. If you have to deviate from *real world* tests, be prepared to explain why.

Lab reports should contain:

1. A description of the analytical techniques used in the tests

2. The quantitative or qualitative results with any appropriate qualifications concerning the degree of certainty surrounding them

3. An explanation of any necessary presumptions or inferences that were needed to reach the conclusions

As the expert, you must perform or witness the tests in person. If you use an independent lab, you must guide and control the tests.

Independent laboratory. Some tests are best run by an independent laboratory because the results will appear to be even more objective and/or because you may not have the required measuring devices. You should specifically describe the tests you want performed.

Select the independent laboratory carefully. Do they have the right equipment and personnel and are they properly accredited? When selecting a facility or running a test, think of how you will present the findings to the jury.

Consider your tests carefully before you run them. If they lead to undesirable results, it is difficult, if not unethical, to delete them from your report and testimony.

If your client-attorney contracts with the laboratory, the laboratory report will become his or her work product and be undiscoverable by the opposition. Another personal advantage of having your client-attorney deal directly with the testing facility is that it keeps you out of the billing chain.

Preliminary laboratory reports from the lab to you should be verbal so that other clarifying tests may be discussed. Preliminary results which may be damaging to the case may be embarrassing (and misleading) if committed to paper before subsequent tests are completed.

The testing facility must never communicate with the opposition. They are working for your side.

Many labs and experts destroy their working notes once their final report is drafted. They feel the final report shows everything reflected in the notes and that there is no further need for the working documents.

Machine calibration. All measuring tools should be calibrated regularly and the calibration should be recorded. If your calipers, voltmeters, etc. are calibrated by an independent service and the measurements can be traced to the National Bureau of Standards, your testimony will be more credible.

When challenging someone else's testing, your client-attorney might ask: *When was this machine last calibrated?*

When you are challenged, you might be able to say: *Calibration is not necessary as the measurements are relative* (comparative) *to each other.*

If testing is expected to be lengthy, you may wish to request 50% of your fee in advance.

After the trial, physical evidence is often secured by the court and cannot be retrieved by the owner or expert. Be prepared to lose anything entered into evidence.

When testing, contact your client-attorney weekly to keep him or her informed.

Legal Evidence Control and Transmittal Form

Case Name:
Client:
Project Number:
Tag Number:
Client-Attorney:
File or Claim Number:
Insurance Company:
Adjuster Company:
Responsible Contact:
Telephone:
Received by:
Received from:
Date:
Witness:
Sampling by:
Description of evidence:

Transferred to:
Date:
Received by:
Witness:
All of above items, only items as follows:

Disposition of evidence:
Not pertinent to case per authority of:
Client contacted for return, rental or disposition by:
Date:
Placed in bonded storage at:
Per authority of:
Date:
Storage number:
Scrapped per authority of:
Date:

Evidence Storage/Disposition Form

(Case name)
To:

Ladies and Gentlemen:

Apex Testing laboratories maintains locked legal storage space for the retention of evidence while actively pursuing the study identified herein. During our study and prior to making a formal report no charge is made for the retention of evidence.

Upon completion of our study, we prefer to return all evidence to our client. We can retain small samples in our legal storage for a fee of $30. per month, billed quarterly and payable in advance. Large items can be transferred to a bonded warehouse.

Your case or file number:

Lab project number:

Lab report number:

Item(s):

Please notify us within thirty (30) days as to your requirements in the disposition of these materials.

Discard:

Return to the attention of:

Transfer to bonded storage:

Retain per rental defined above. $ _____ Payment enclosed.

Authorization:

Failure to respond will initiate disposal of the materials mentioned above.
By:

CHAPTER FIFTEEN

Your Curriculum Vita

Your curriculum vita is your resume. It lists your education, job history, articles or books you have published—everything pertinent to your field of expertise. You send it to attorneys who call you about working on a case. They will use your CV to evaluate your qualifications.

Your CV should deal only with one area of expertise. If you are working in two separate and unrelated fields, such as bicycle mechanics and mountain climbing, for example, draft a CV for each. Although many people think parachutes and Para-Sails are nearly identical, they are not. Separate CVs are in order.

Some people like to use their word processor to tailor their CV to the case at hand.

Your CV must be honest and accurate. Your client-attorney and the opposing attorney will probably check your background. You do not want to be exposed as a fraud on the witness stand.

CVs are usually entered into evidence and go into the jury room with the other evidence. You want to leave a lasting impression; your CV should talk for you long after you have left the stand.

The proper length for your CV is debatable. A long CV makes you look important but leaves more for the opposing attorney to question. Some experts like to publish a long CV for their attorney and a shorter, tailored CV for the opposition. This is not difficult if you maintain a long draft in your word processor and then edit out the extraneous material to provide a customized edition for the deposition.

Sit down at the keyboard and start building your CV. Place your name and field of specialty at the top and then list your:

- Certifications and licenses

- Education and training, formal and on the job

- Professional affiliations and memberships

- Chronological work experience

- Publications such as books and articles

- Patents held, if any

- Awards

Use a separate paragraph for each item on the list. Print out the CV on your letterhead.

Then, in a second section of the document, list everything pertinent you have done in this field since leaving school, year by year. As you work on the second section, more ideas will come to you for use in the first section. Keep building, researching and digging into your files. This takes time but the result is very impressive and you will use it again and again.

Print out a clean copy for your file. Reproduce it as needed, either on the word processor or a good, clean photocopy machine. Use high quality paper to create a good impression.

The hiring attorney wants to know how you will look in court, so include a photo of yourself properly dressed. A wallet sized photo can be pasted to the CV. They are fairly inexpensive when ordered in quantity. Color always sells better than black and white.

Do not fold your CV, fee schedule and other materials. Mail them in a flat 9 x 12 envelope. Make them easy to handle and file.

(Letterhead)

Robert A. Katz: Aircraft Accident Reconstruction

Updated January 1, 1988

Certifications
Professional Engineer, Safety (California) SF–0002
Certified Safety Professional No. 590062

Education and Training
BS - University of Massachusetts, 1962
MS - University of Southern California, 1965
Pilot training, U.S. Air Force, 1966
USAF Flight Safety School, University of California, 1967
Aircraft Crash Survival Investigation School, ASU, 1968

Professional Affiliations
American Society of Safety Engineers Member
Systems Safety Society, President 1970–1972
U.S. Parachute Association, Secretary 1973–1974

Professional Experience
1984–Present: Faculty, University of California, Institute of Safety and Systems Management. Lecturing in Aircraft Accident Investigation, Safety Engineering, and Safety Program Management.

1970–1984: Vice–President, Engineering, U.S. Aviation Corp.

1968–1970: Chief of Safety Policy and Programs, U.S. Air Force, Directorate of Aerospace Safety.

1966–1968: Aviation Accident Investigation, Hickam AFB, Hawaii.

Flying Experience
Pilot. Commercial License. 8,700 hours.
1,200 parachute jumps, Master Parachute Rigger, Instructor.

Professional Papers and Research
Over 400 articles, most in a monthly column in *Aircraft Safety* Magazine
Five books on flying and aircraft safety including *The Cat and Duck Method of Instrument Flying.*
Other publications on request.

Curriculum Vita example

CHAPTER SIXTEEN

Your List of Cases

It is useful to maintain a list of the cases you have worked on. The list will reveal several things to you once it starts to grow. How many cases have you taken part in? What percentage went to trial? Do you have a good balance of cases for the plaintiff and defense? Have you worked for the same firm several times? What year did you begin expert witness work?

Generally, your list of cases is for your own use though your client-attorney may be interested in the information. It is not something you want opposing attorneys to find. They could use it to research all your past cases and try to find conflicting testimony to impeach you.

One aviation safety consultant keeps a computer record in dBASE III + with the following fields: date file was opened, title of case, date of accident, type of aircraft, registration of aircraft, plaintiff or defendant, client firm, primary consultant (if there is more than one person working in your firm), court, win/loss/settle, and date case was closed. Kept in the computer, the information is easy to update and print out. Searching and grouping is also simplified.

CHAPTER SEVENTEEN

Jury Selection

Before the jury is selected. You probably have more experience in cases in your particular field than your client-attorney. You certainly know more about your subject and how different types of people perceive it. You want a group of jurors who are more likely to identify and sympathize with your side. Brief your attorney.

There are consulting firms that specialize in jury evaluation. They perform background checks and observe the reactions of potential jurors during voir dire (the educating and challenging process of selecting a jury). Most of the cases you work on will not be large enough to warrant this service. It will be up to you to suggest general guidelines to your client-attorney.

Almost every potential juror has some form of expertise. A problem arises when one juror knows something about your area of specialty. The jurors are more likely to ask this juror-expert for advice and the new-found power could go to his or her head. As a result, you now have a jury of one — and that one may not like you.

For example, in a parachute case, you do not want to include pilots on the jury. Pilots are horizontal aviators while skydivers are engaged in vertical aviation. Many pilots fear and/or dislike air traffic that might collide with their aircraft. Some pilots have a high opinion of themselves and feel that their type of aviation is the only legitimate kind. To compound the problem, other jurors are likely to defer to the pilot for guidance in aviation matters. So, your whole case may turn on the reaction of one juror instead of the social dynamics among several.

On the other hand, female homemakers may make good jurors in parachute cases. Many of them sew. They understand fabric and stitching. When you show them the parachute and point to the construction, they will move to the front of their seats and nod their heads.

Think about your area of expertise and make a list of the types of jurors you would like (and not like) to include. Tell your client-attorney so that he or she will be particularly sensitive to these characteristics in potential jurors during the voir dire.

After the jury is selected. Once your jury is selected, consider what you want to show them. Is this an urban or rural trial? What is the racial makeup? Mostly male or female?

In a rural trial, the jury may not warm up to an out-of-town expert. Many attorneys like to get a local academic type for the lead expert, then call you in for specific expert testimony.

If the jury is largely Hispanic, suggest the client send the Hispanic vice-president to represent the company rather than the Anglo sales manager.

In very conservative areas, Utah for example, female experts may find their job more difficult.

For more information, see the excellent book *What Makes Juries Listen* by Sonya Hamlin. Details are in the Appendix.

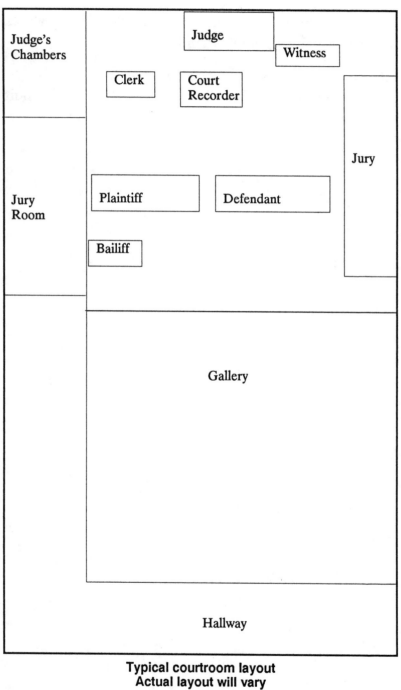

Typical courtroom layout
Actual layout will vary

CHAPTER EIGHTEEN

A Guide to the Law and the Courts

This chapter will help you understand points of law, courtroom procedures, criminal actions, legal transactions, and arrest procedures. In short, it is a lay guide to the law and the courts. It traces the steps normally involved in a civil case and a criminal case, explaining the procedures most common to most of them. Keep in mind that some variations of procedure exist among the various state courts and even among federal courts.

This chapter contains a condensation of *Law and the Courts*: A Layman's Handbook of Court Procedures, and is reprinted by permission of the American Bar Association. The complete booklet is available for $2.00 postpaid from the ABA, Circulation Department, 750 North Lake Shore Drive, Chicago, IL 60611. Copyright © 1980, American Bar Association.

Civil cases

How a Lawsuit Begins. Court actions fall into two broad categories — civil and criminal. Civil cases are those in which an individual, business or agency of government seeks damages or relief from another individual, business or agency of government; these constitute the great bulk of cases in the courts. The most common example is the suit for damages arising from an automobile accident. A criminal action is one by the state or federal government against an individual charged with committing a crime.

This section deals with an average civil case. Civil actions generally are brought for breach of contract (*ex contractu*), or for a wrong (*ex delicto*) or tort.

In the early days of the law, courts and lawyers were inclined to restrict the scope of legal actions. Thus, if a set of facts did not fit into an established legal "pigeon hole", the client was without remedy even though he had suffered a wrong to his person or property.

As a consequence, a new system — equity — evolved which provides a remedy that previously was not available. Equity covers such matters as preventing the continuance of a wrong (injunction), and compelling the performance of a contract to sell real estate or unique personal property (specific performance). Ordinarily neither a jury trial nor money damages can be obtained in equity proceedings.

A person who believes that he has been injured or damaged by another person or business firm consults his lawyer and tells him the facts and circumstances which he believes constitute a cause of legal action. The attorney takes the client's statement, interviews possible witnesses, examines applicable statutes and court decisions, and tries to determine whether the client has a case.

If the attorney concludes the client does have a cause of action, he prepares and files a *complaint* or *petition* in the proper court. His client is the *plaintiff* and the person or firm against whom the case is filed is the *defendant*.

The petition states the facts of the plaintiff's action against the defendant and sets forth the damages, judgment or other relief sought. However, the mere filing of a suit is not proof that the plaintiff has a cause of action. Later events may demonstrate that his claim is invalid.

The attorney for the plaintiff also files with the clerk of the court a *praecipe for a summons*. This is a request for the court clerk to issue a *summons* or notice, and to direct the county sheriff to serve a copy of it on the defendant. In some states, a praecipe is not necessary and the summons is issued as a matter of course. In others, the summons may be served in advance of the filing of the petition or complaint. In still others, any person over 21 and not a party to the action may serve the summons.

After the sheriff has served the summons, he returns the original of the summons to the court, with a notation as to whether and, if so, how the defendant was served with the summons. Serving of the summons is the defendant's formal notification of suit. Filing a complaint and serving the summons commences the case.

After service, the defendant is entitled to a certain period of time within which to file his *pleading,* or answer, to the plaintiff's petition.

Jurisdiction and Venue. The attorney must select the proper county or district in which to file the case. A court has no authority to render a judgment in any case unless it has *jurisdiction* over the person or property involved. This means that the court must be able to exercise control over the defendant, or that the property involved must be located in the county or district under the court's control.

Certain actions are said to be *local — that is, they may be brought only in the county where the subject matter of the litigation is located. An example of a local action would be an action for the foreclosure of a mortgage on real estate.*

Other actions are said to be *transitory* — that is, they may be brought in any county in any state where the defendant may be found and served with summons. An action for personal injuries is an example of a transitory action.

Venue means the county or district where the action is to be tried. Venue may be changed to another county or district upon application or by agreement. Where wide prejudicial publicity has been given to a case before trial, a change of venue is sometimes sought in an effort to secure jurors who have not formed an opinion or to provide a neutral forum not charged with local bias. Venue also may be changed to serve the convenience of witnesses.

A *change of venue from the judge* usually is granted on an application, which claims that the judge has some relationship to the parties, attorneys or facts of the case, which prevents his being completely unbiased during the trial.

Preparation for Trial. The plaintiff and defendant, through their respective attorneys, attempt to marshall all of the pertinent facts bearing upon the case. The defendant may begin his defense by filing certain pleadings, which may include one or more of the following:

Motion to Quash Service of Summons. Questions whether the defendant has been properly served with summons, as provided by law.

Motion to Strike. Asks the court to rule whether the plaintiff's petition contains irrelevant, prejudicial or other improper matter. If it does, the court may order such matter deleted.

Motion to Make More Definite and Certain. Asks the court to require the plaintiff to set out the facts of his complaint more specifically, or to describe his injury or damages in greater detail, so that the defendant can answer more precisely.

Motion to Dismiss. Asks the court to rule that the plaintiff's complaint does not state a legally sound cause of action against the defendant even if, for the purpose of the motion, the defendant admits that all the facts set out by the plaintiff are true. This was once called a *demurrer.*

Answer. This statement by the defendant denies the allegations in the plaintiff's petition, or admits some and denies others, or admits all and pleads an excuse.

Cross-petition or Cross-complaint. May be filed by the defendant either separately or as part of his answer. It asks for relief or damages on the part of the defendant against the original plaintiff, and perhaps others. When a cross-petition is filed, the plaintiff may then file any of the previously-mentioned motions to the cross-petition, except a motion to quash service of summons.

Reply. Either party in the case may file a reply, which constitutes an answer to any new allegations raised by the other party in prior pleadings.

Note: A *plea* or *pleading* refers to an answer or other formal document filed in the action. The words should not be used to describe an argument made in court by a lawyer.

Taking of Depositions. A *deposition* is an out-of-court statement of a witness under oath, intended for use in court or in preparation for trial. Under prevailing statutes and rules in most jurisdictions, either of the parties in a civil action may take the deposition of the other party, or of any witness.

Depositions frequently are necessary to preserve the testimony of important witnesses who cannot appear in court or who reside in another state or jurisdiction. This might be the testimony of a friendly witness — one whose evidence is considered helpful to the plaintiff or defendant, as the case may be. Or it might involve an adverse witness whose statements are taken, by one side or the other, to determine the nature of the evidence he would give if summoned as a witness in the trial.

The deposition may take the form of answers to written questions or of oral examination followed by cross-examination.

A deposition is not a public record, and not available to the press until it is made so by court order.

A state may not compel the presence at a civil trial of a witness who is outside the state or who is in another county of the same state. When the testimony of such a witness is sought, the procedure is for the party seeking the testimony to apply to the court in which the case is pending for the issuance of a commission — commonly called *letters rogatory*. This is directed to an official or attorney in the jurisdiction where the witness is, empowering him to take the witness's deposition and forward it to the court.

In some states, it is not necessary to secure the issuance of a commission, but only to serve notice of the taking of the deposition upon opposing attorneys.

If a witness is absent from the jurisdiction or is unable to attend the trial in person, his deposition may be read in evidence. If a person who has given a deposition also appears as a witness at the trial, his deposition may be used to attack his credibility, if his oral testimony at the trial is inconsistent with that contained in the deposition.

Discovery. In addition to taking depositions in an attempt to ascertain the facts upon which another party relies, either party may submit written questions, called *interrogatories*, to the other party and require that such be answered under oath.

Other methods of discovery are: requiring adverse parties to produce books, records and documents for inspection, to submit to a physical examination, or to admit or deny the genuineness of documents.

Pre-Trial Conference. After all the pleadings of both parties have been filed and the case is *at issue,* many courts then set the case for a pre-trial hearing. At this hearing, the attorneys appear, generally without their clients and, in the presence of the judge, seek to agree on undisputed facts, called *stipulations.* These may include such matters as time and place in the case of an accident, the use of pictures, maps or sketches, and other matters, including points of law.

The objective of the pre-trial hearing is to shorten the actual trial time without infringing upon the rights of either party.

Pre-trial procedure, used extensively in the federal district courts, frequently results in the settlement of the case without trial. If it does not, the court assigns a specific trial date for the case, following the pre-trial hearing.

Criminal Cases

Bringing the Charge. Criminal charges are instituted against an individual in one of two ways:

1) Through an *indictment*, or true bill, voted by a grand jury, or

2) Through the filing of an *information* in court by the prosecuting attorney (sometimes called the county, district or state's attorney), alleging the commission of a crime.

In either case, the charge must set forth the time, date and place of the alleged criminal act as well as the nature of the charge.

In most states, crimes of a serious nature, such as murder or treason, may be charged by indictment only. In some states, the prosecutor has the option in any case to proceed by way of indictment or information.

The Grand Jury. The grand jury is a body of citizens (usually 16, but varying in number from state to state) summoned by the court to inquire into crimes committed in the county or, in the case of federal grand juries, in the federal court district.

Grand jury proceedings are private and secret. Prospective defendants are not entitled to be present at the proceedings, and no one appears to cross-examine witnesses on the defendant's behalf.

However, a witness before a federal grand jury is free to describe his testimony to anyone he pleases, after he leaves the grand jury room. To this extent, such proceedings are not secret.

Although all states have provision for impaneling a grand jury, only about half use it as a regular arm of law enforcement. In the others, the prosecutor, on his own responsibility, is empowered to make formal accusation of all, or of all but the most serious, crimes.

In states where the grand jury is utilized, it is convened at regular intervals, or it may be impaneled at special times by the court to consider important cases.

The grand jury has broad investigative powers: it may compel the attendance of witnesses; require the taking of oaths; and compel answers to questions and the submission of records.

Ordinarily, however, the grand jury hears only such witnesses as the prosecutor calls before it and considers only the cases presented to it by the prosecutor.

Nevertheless, a grand jury may undertake inquiries of its own, in effect taking the initiative away from the prosecutor. In common parlance, this is known as a *runaway* grand jury.

The grand jury's traditional function is to determine whether information elicited by the prosecutor, or by its own inquiries, is adequate to warrant the return of an indictment or true bill charging a person or persons with a particular crime. If the grand jury concludes that the evidence does not warrant a formal charge, it may return a *no bill.*

In several states, powers of investigation similar to those of the grand jury are conferred by law upon a single person, a judicial officer or a deputy appointed by him, known as *a one man grand jury.*

Arrest Procedure. When an indictment is returned by a grand jury, or an information is filed by the prosecuting attorney, the clerk of the court issues a *warrant* for the arrest of the person charged, if he has not already been arrested and taken into custody.

The law usually requires in a *felony* case (generally, a crime for which a person may be confined in the penitentiary) that the defendant must promptly be brought before a magistrate or justice of the peace (in federal cases, the U.S. Commissioner) and be permitted to post bond, in order to secure release from custody, and either request or waive a *preliminary hearing.* When the grand jury indicts, there is no preliminary hearing. In most states, however, persons charged with murder are not eligible for release on a bail bond.

Many jurisdictions permit law enforcement officials to hold a person without formal charge up to 24 hours for the purpose of investigation. But he may not be held for an unreasonable time unless a criminal charge is filed. In addition, the defendant formally charged with a crime is entitled to an attorney at all times. If he is unable to procure an attorney and if he requests counsel, the court will appoint an attorney to represent him, at public expense and without cost to him.

Preliminary Hearing. If the individual charged with a crime requests a preliminary hearing before a magistrate, the court will set a hearing within a reasonably short time. At the hearing, the state must present sufficient evidence to convince the magistrate that there is reason to believe the defendant has committed the crime with which he is charged. The defendant must be present at this hearing, and he may or may not present evidence on his own behalf.

If the magistrate believes the evidence justifies it, he will order the defendant *bound over* for trial in the proper court—that is, placed under bond for appearance at trial, or held in jail if the charge involved is not a bailable offense or if the defendant is unable to post bond. The magistrate also may decide that even without bond the accused will most likely appear in court for his trial and therefore will release him on his *own recognizance;* that is, on his own promise to appear. If he concludes that the state has failed to produce sufficient evidence in the preliminary hearing, the magistrate may dismiss the charge and order the defendant released.

Arraignment. In most instances, a criminal case is placed on the court's calendar for *arraignment.* On the date fixed, the accused appears, the indictment or information is read to him, his rights are explained by the judge, and he is asked whether he pleads *guilty* or *not guilty* to the charge.

If he pleads not guilty, his case will be set later for trial; if he pleads guilty, his case ordinarily will be set later for sentencing. In cases of minor offenses, sentences may be imposed immediately. But in some states, arraignment and plea are separate proceedings, held on different days.

Preparation for Trial. As in civil cases, very careful preparation on the part of the state and the defense precedes the trial. However, the defense may first enter a motion challenging the jurisdiction of the court over the particular offense involved, or over the particular defendant. The defense attorney also may file a *demurrer*, or motion for dismissal, as in a civil suit.

In preparing for trial, attorneys for both sides will interview prospective witnesses and, if deemed necessary, secure expert evidence, and gather testimony concerning ballistics, chemical tests, cases and other similar data.

Pre-Trial Settlement. Most cases are settled prior to trial. In civil cases, settlement is one of the objectives of the pre-trial conference. In complex civil cases, special settlement conferences may be held.

Many criminal charges are terminated by plea negotiations in which a defendant enters a plea of guilty or nolo contendere in the expectation that other charges will be dismissed or that sentence concessions will be granted.

Some communities have experimental programs for removing some controversies from court altogether, as through use of arbitration or mediation in facilities such as neighborhood justice centers.

Trials, Civil or Criminal.

While in detail there are minor differences in trial procedure between civil and criminal cases, the basic pattern in the courtroom is the same. Consequently, this section treats the trial steps collectively.

Officers of the Court. The *judge* is the officer who is either elected or appointed to preside over the court. If the case is tried before a jury, the judge rules upon points of law dealing with trial procedure, presentation of the evidence and the law of the case. If the case is tried before the judge alone, he will determine the facts in addition to performing the aforementioned duties.

The *court clerk* is an officer of the court, also either elected or appointed who, at the beginning of the trial, upon the judge's instruction, gives the entire panel of prospective jurors (*veniremen*) an oath. By this oath, the venireman promises that, if called, he will truly answer any question concerning his qualifications to sit as a juror in the case.

Any venireman who is disqualified by law, or has a valid reason to be excused under the law, ordinarily is excused by the judge at this time. A person may be disqualified from jury duty because he is not a resident voter or householder, because of age, hearing defects, or because he has served recently on a jury.

Then the court clerk will draw names of the remaining veniremen from a box, and they will take seats in the jury box. After twelve veniremen have been approved as jurors by the judge and the attorneys, the court clerk will administer an oath to the persons so chosen to *well and truly try the case*.

The *bailiff* is an officer of the court whose duties are to keep order in the courtroom, to call witnesses, and to take charge of the jury as instructed by the court at such times as the jury may not be in the courtroom, and particularly when, having received the case, the jury is deliberating upon its decision. It is the duty of the bailiff to see that no one talks with or attempts to influence the jurors in any manner.

The *court recorder* has the duty of recording all proceedings in the courtroom, including testimony of the witnesses, objections made to evidence by the attorneys and the rulings of the court thereon, and listing and marking for identification any exhibits offered or introduced into evidence. In some states, the clerk of the court has charge of exhibits.

The *attorneys* are officers of the court whose duties are to represent their respective clients and present the evidence on their behalf, so that the jury or the judge may reach a just verdict or decision.

The role of the attorney is sometimes misunderstood, particularly in criminal proceedings. Our system of criminal jurisprudence presumes every defendant to be innocent until proved guilty beyond a *reasonable doubt.* Every defendant is entitled to be represented by legal counsel, regardless of the unpopularity of his cause. This is a constitutional safeguard.

It is entirely ethical for an attorney to represent a defendant whom the community may assume to be guilty. The accused is entitled to counsel in order that he be protected from conviction on insufficient evidence, and he is entitled to every protection which the law affords him.

Jury List. The trial jury in either a civil or criminal case is called a *petit jury.* It is chosen by lot by the court clerk from a previously compiled list called a venire or, in some places, the *jury array.*

The methods of selecting names of persons for the venire vary among court jurisdictions. The lists in many states are comprised of tax assessment rolls or voter registration lists.

The law in many states requires a preliminary screening by a court official to eliminate persons unqualified or ineligible under the provisions of applicable state laws. In the federal courts, the court clerk is assisted in compiling the list by a *jury commissioner* appointed by the presiding judge.

Some people may be exempted from jury duty by reason of their occupations. These exemptions differ from state to state, but in some jurisdictions those automatically exempted include lawyers, physicians, dentists, pharmacists, teachers, and clergymen. In a number of others, nurses, journalists, printers, railroad, telephone and telegraph employees, government officials, firemen and policemen are among the exempt occupational groups.

On the other hand, many courts are excusing fewer prospective jurors today.

On occasion, the qualification of all jurors may be challenged. This is called a *challenge to the array* and generally is based on the allegation that the officers charged with selecting the jurors did so in an illegal manner.

Selecting the Jury. In most cases, a jury of twelve is required in either a civil or criminal proceeding. In some states, a jury of six may be used for certain trials. In some courts, alternate jurors are selected to take the places of members of the regular panel who may become disabled during the trial. These alternate jurors hear the evidence just as do the regular jurors, but do not participate in the deliberations unless a regular juror or jurors become disabled.

The jury selection begins with the calling by the court clerk of twelve veniremen, whose names are selected at random, to take their places in the jury enclosure. The attorneys for the parties, or sometimes the judge, may then make a brief statement of the facts involved, for the purpose of acquainting the jurors with sufficient facts so that they may intelligently answer the questions put to them by the judge and the attorneys. The questions elicit information, such as the name, the occupation, the place of business and residence of the prospective juror, and any personal knowledge he may have of the case. This questioning of the jurors is known as the *voir dire.*

If the venireman expresses an opinion or prejudice which will affect his judgment in the case, the court will dismiss him *for cause,* and a substitute juror will be called by the court clerk. There is no limit on the number of veniremen who may be excused *for cause.*

In addition to the challenges for cause, each party has the right to exercise a specific number of *peremptory challenges.* This permits an attorney to excuse a particular juror without having to state a cause. If a peremptory challenge is exercised, another juror then is called until attorneys on both sides have exercised all of the peremptory challenges permitted by law, or they have waived further challenges. The number of peremptory challenges is limited and varies with the type of case.

Thus, the jury is selected and then is sworn in by the court clerk to try the case. The remaining members of the jury panel are excused and directed to report to another court in session at the time.

Not all trials have juries. In some cases, due to the subject matter of the trial, there is no right to a jury. Also, the right to a jury trial may be waived in individual cases.

Separating the Witnesses. In certain cases, civil or criminal, the attorney on either side may advise the court that he is *calling for the rule* on witnesses. This means that, except for the plaintiff or complaining witness and the defendant, all witnesses who may testify for either party will be excluded from the courtroom until they are called to testify. These witnesses are admonished by the judge not to discuss the case or their testimony with other witnesses or persons, except the attorneys. This is sometimes called *separation of witnesses* or *sequestration*. If the rule is not called for, the witnesses may remain in the courtroom if they desire.

Opening Statements. After selection of the jury, the plaintiff's attorney, or attorney for the state in a criminal case, may make an opening statement to advise the jury what he intends to prove in the case. This statement must be confined to facts intended to be elicited in evidence and cannot be argumentative. The attorney for the defendant also may make an opening statement for the same purpose or, in some states, may reserve the opening statement until the end of the plaintiff's or state's case. Either party may waive his opening statement if he desires.

Presentation of Evidence. The plaintiff in a civil case, or the state in a criminal case, will begin the presentation of evidence with their *witnesses*. These usually will include the plaintiff in a civil case, although they are not required to testify.

A witness may testify to a matter of fact. He can tell what he saw, heard (unless it is hearsay as explained below), felt, smelled or touched through the use of his physical senses.

A witness also may be used to identify documents, pictures or other physical exhibits in the trial.

Generally, he cannot state his opinion or give his conclusion unless he is an expert or especially qualified to do so. In some instances, a witness may be permitted to express an opinion, for example, as to the speed an auto was traveling or whether a person was intoxicated.

A witness who has been qualified in a particular field as an *expert* may give his opinion based upon the facts in evidence and may state the reasons for that opinion. Sometimes the facts in evidence are put to the expert in a question called a *hypothetical question*. The question assumes the truth of the facts contained in it. Other times, an expert is asked to state an opinion based on personal knowledge of the facts through his own examination or investigation.

Generally, a witness cannot testify to *hearsay*; that is, what someone else has told him outside the presence of the parties to the action.

Also, a witness is not permitted to testify about matters that are too remote to have any bearing on the decision of the case, or matters that are irrelevant or immaterial.

Usually, an attorney may not ask *leading questions* of his own witness, although an attorney is sometimes allowed to elicit routine, noncontroversial information. A leading question is one which suggests the answer desired.

Objections may be made by the opposing counsel to leading questions, or to questions that call for an opinion or conclusion on the part of the witness, or require an answer based on hearsay. There are many other reasons for objections under the rules of evidence.

Objections are often made in the following form: *I object to that question on the ground that it is irrelevant and immaterial and for the further reason that it calls for an opinion and conclusion of the witness.* Many jurisdictions require that the objection specify why the question is not proper.

The judge will thereupon sustain or deny the objection. If sustained, another question must then be asked, or the same question be rephrased in proper form.

If an objection to a question is sustained on either direct or cross-examination, the attorney asking the question may make an *offer to prove*. This offer is dictated to the court reporter away from the hearing of the jury. In it, the attorney states the answer which the witness would have given if permitted. The offer forms part of the record if the case is subsequently appealed.

If the objection is overruled, the witness may then answer. The attorney who made the objection may thereupon take an *exception*, which simply means that he is preserving a record so that, if the case is appealed, he may argue that the court erred in overruling the objection. In some states, the rules permit an automatic exception to an adverse ruling without its being asked for in each instance.

Cross-Examination. When plaintiff's attorney or the state's attorney has finished his direct examination of the witness, the defendant's attorney or opposing counsel may then cross-examine the witness on any matter about which the witness has been questioned initially in direct examination. The cross-examining attorney may ask leading questions for the purpose of inducing the witness to testify about matters which he may otherwise have chosen to ignore.

On cross-examination, the attorney may try to bring out prejudice or bias of the witness, such as his relationship or friendship to the party, or other interest in the case. The witness can be asked if he has been convicted of a felony or crime involving moral turpitude, since this bears upon his credibility.

The plaintiff's attorney may object to certain questions asked on cross-examination on previously mentioned grounds or because they deal with facts not touched upon in direct examination.

Re-Direct Examination. After the opposing attorney is finished with his cross-examination, the attorney who called the witness has the right to ask questions on *re-direct examination.* The re-direct examination covers new matters brought out in cross-examination and generally is an effort to rehabilitate a witness whose testimony on direct examination has been weakened by cross-examination.

Then the opposing attorney may re-cross-examine.

Demurrer to Plaintiff's or State's Case, or Motion for Directed Verdict. At the conclusion of the plaintiff's or state's evidence, the attorney will announce that the plaintiff or state *rests.*

Then, away from the presence of the jury, the defendant's counsel may *demur* to the plaintiff's or state's case on the ground that a cause of action or that the commission of a crime has not been proven. In many states, this is known as a *motion for a directed verdict;* that is, a verdict which the judge orders the jury to return.

The judge will either sustain or overrule the demurrer or motion. If it is sustained, the case is concluded. If it is overruled, the defendant then is given the opportunity to present his evidence.

Presentation of Evidence by the Defendant. The defense attorney may elect to present no evidence, or may present certain evidence but not place the defendant upon the stand.

In a criminal case, the defendant need not take the stand unless he wishes to do so. The defendant has constitutional protection against self-incrimination. He is not required to prove his innocence. The plaintiff or the state has the *burden of proof.*

In a civil case, the plaintiff must prove his case by a *preponderance of the evidence.* This means the greater weight of the evidence.

The defendant is presumed to be not negligent or liable in a civil case, and not guilty in a criminal case.

The defense attorney may feel that the burden of proof has not been sustained, or that presentation of the defendant's witnesses might strengthen the plaintiff's case. If the defendant does present evidence, he does so in the same manner as the plaintiff or the state, as described above, and the plaintiff or state will cross-examine the defendant's witnesses.

Rebuttal Evidence. At the conclusion of the defendant's case, the plaintiff or state's attorney may then present rebuttal witnesses or evidence designed to refute the testimony and evidence presented by the defendant. The matter covered is evidence on which the plaintiff or state did not present evidence in its *case in chief* initially; or it may be a new witness to contradict the defendant's witness. If there is a so-called *surprise witness,* this is often where you will find him.

After rebuttal evidence, the defendant may present additional evidence to contradict it.

Final Motions. At the conclusion of all the evidence, the defendant may again renew his demurrer or motion for directed verdict. The motion is made away from the presence of the jury. If the demurrer or motion is sustained, the case is concluded. If overruled, the trial proceeds.

Thus, the case has now been concluded on the evidence, and it is ready to be submitted to the jury.

Conferences During the Trial. Occasionally during the trial, the lawyers will ask permission to approach the bench and speak to the judge, or the judge may call them to the bench. They whisper about admissibility of certain evidence, irregularities in the trial or other matters. The judge and lawyers speak in inaudible tones because the jurors might be prejudiced by what they hear. The question of admissibility of evidence is a matter of law for the judge, not the jury, to decide. If the ruling cannot be made quickly, the judge will order the jury to retire, and will hear the attorneys' arguments outside the jury's presence.

Whenever the jury leaves the courtroom, the judge will admonish them not to form or express an opinion or discuss the case with anyone.

Closing Arguments. The attorney for the plaintiff or state will present the first argument in closing the case. Generally, he will summarize and comment on the evidence in the most favorable light for his side. He may talk about the facts and properly drawn inferences.

He cannot talk about issues outside the case or about evidence that was not presented. He is not allowed to comment on the defendant's failure to take the stand as a witness in a criminal case.

If he does talk about improper matters, the opposing attorney may object, and the judge will rule on the objection. If the offending remarks are deemed seriously prejudicial, the opposing attorney will ask that the jury be instructed to disregard them, and in some instances may move for a *mistrial,* that is, ask that the present trial be terminated and the case be set for retrial at a later date.

Ordinarily, before closing arguments, the judge will indicate to the attorneys the instructions he will give the jury, and it is proper for the attorneys in closing argument to comment on them and to relate them to the evidence.

The defendant's attorney will next present his arguments. He usually answers statements made in opening argument, points out defects in the plaintiff's case, and summarizes the facts favorable to his client.

Then the plaintiff or state is entitled to the concluding argument to answer the defendant's argument and to make a final appeal to the jury. The plaintiff or state gets the last word because it has the burden of proof.

If the defendant chooses not to make a closing argument, which sometimes occurs, then the plaintiff or state loses the right to the last argument.

Instructions to the Jury. Although giving instructions to the jury is the function of the judge, in many states attorneys for each side submit a number of instructions designed to apply the law to the facts in evidence. The judge will indicate which instructions he will accept and which he will refuse. The attorneys may make objections to such rulings for the purpose of the record in any appeal.

The judge reads these instructions to the jury. This is commonly referred to as the judge's *charge* to the jury. The instructions cover the law as applicable to the case.

In most cases, only the judge may determine what the law is. In some states, however, the jurors in criminal cases are judges of both the facts and the law.

In giving the instructions, the judge will state the issues in the case and define any terms or words necessary. He will tell the jury what it must decide on the issues, if it is to find for the plaintiff or state, or for the defendant. He will advise the jury that it is the sole judge of the facts and of the credibility of witnesses; that upon leaving the courtroom to reach a verdict, it must elect a *foreman* of the jury and then reach a decision based upon the judgment of each individual juror. In some states, the first juror chosen automatically becomes the foreman.

In the Jury Room. After the instructions, the bailiff will take the jury to the jury room to begin deliberations.

The bailiff will sit outside and not permit anyone to enter or leave the jury room. No one may attempt to *tamper* with the jury in any way while it is deliberating.

Ordinarily, the court furnishes the jury with written forms of all possible verdicts so that when a decision is reached, the jury can choose the proper verdict form.

The decision will be signed by the foreman of the jury and be returned to the courtroom. Ordinarily, the decision in a criminal case must be unanimous. In some jurisdictions, in civil cases, only nine or ten out of twelve jurors need agree to reach a verdict. However, all federal courts require a unanimous verdict.

If the jurors cannot agree on a verdict, the jury is called a *hung jury*, and the case may be retried before a new jury at a later date.

In some states, the jury may take the judge's instructions and the exhibits introduced in evidence to the jury room.

If necessary, the jury may return to the courtroom in the presence of counsel to ask a question of the judge about his instructions. In such instances, the judge may reread all or certain of the instructions previously given, or supplement or clarify them by further instructions.

If the jury is out overnight, the members often will be housed in a hotel and secluded from all contacts with other persons. In many cases, the jury will be excused to go home at night, especially if there is no objection by either party.

Verdict. Upon reaching a verdict, the jury returns to the courtroom with the bailiff and, in the presence of the judge, the parties and their respective attorneys, the verdict is read or announced aloud in open court. The reading or announcement may be made by the jury foreman or the court clerk.

Attorneys for either party, but usually the losing party, may ask that the jury be *polled*, in which case each individual juror will be asked if the verdict is his verdict. It is rare for a juror to say that it is not his verdict. When the verdict is read and accepted by the court, the jury is dismissed, and the trial is concluded.

Motions After Verdict. Motions permitted to be made after the verdict is rendered will vary from state to state.

A *motion in arrest of judgment* attacks the sufficiency of the indictment or information in a criminal case.

A *motion for judgment non obstante veredicto* may be made after the verdict and before the judgment. This motion requests the judge to enter a judgment for one party, notwithstanding the verdict of the jury in favor of the other side. Ordinarily, this motion raises the same questions as could be raised by a motion for directed verdict.

A *motion for a new trial* sets out alleged errors committed in the trial and asks the trial judge to grant a new trial. In some states, the losing party must make a motion for a new trial before appealing the verdict.

Judgment. The verdict of the jury is ineffective until the judge enters *judgment* upon the verdict. In a civil damage action, this judgment might read: *It is, therefore, ordered, adjudged and decreed that the plaintiff do have and recover the sum of $1,000 of and from the defendant.*

At the request of the plaintiff's lawyer, the clerk of court in such a case will deliver a paper called an *execution* to the sheriff, commanding him to take and sell the property of the defendant and apply the proceeds to the amount of the judgment.

Sentencing. In a criminal case, if the defendant is convicted, the judge will set a date for sentencing. At that time, the judge may consider mitigating facts in determining the appropriate sentence as well as facts about the defendant developed in a pre-sentence investigation.

In the great majority of states and in the federal courts, the function of imposing sentence is exclusively that of the judge. But in some states the jury is called upon to determine the sentence or make sentencing recommendations to the judge for some, or all, crimes.

Rights of Appeal. In a civil case, either party may appeal to a higher court. But in a criminal case, although the defendant has a right to appeal, the prosecution may have no such right or a very limited right to appeal depending upon state law. Appeals in either civil or criminal cases may be on such grounds as errors in trial procedure and errors in *substantive law* — that is, in the interpretation of the law by the trial judge. These are the most common grounds for appeals to higher courts, although there are others.

The prosecution may not appeal in a criminal case if new evidence of defendant's guilt is discovered after his acquittal. Moreover, the state is powerless to bring the defendant to trial again on the same charge. The U.S. and most state constitutions prevent retrial under provisions known as *double jeopardy* clauses.

Criminal defendants have a further appellate safeguard. Those convicted in state courts may appeal to the federal courts on grounds of violation of constitutional rights, if such grounds exist. This privilege serves to impose the powerful check of the federal judicial system upon abuses that may occur in state criminal proceedings.

The record on appeal consists of the papers filed in the trial court and the court reporter's transcript of the evidence. The latter is called a *bill of exceptions* or *transcript on appeal* and must be certified by the trial judge as true and correct. In most states, only as much of the record need be included as will properly present the questions to be raised on appeal.

Appeal. Statutes or rules of court provide for procedure on appeals. Ordinarily, the party appealing is called the *appellant*, and the other party the *appellee*.

The appeal is initiated by filing the transcript of the trial court record with the appellate court within the time prescribed. This filing marks the beginning of the time period within which the appellant must file his *brief* setting forth the reasons and the law upon which he relies in seeking a reversal of the trial court.

The appellee then has a specified time within which to file his answer brief. Following this, the appellant may file a second brief, or brief in reply to the appellee's brief.

When the appeal has been fully briefed, the case may be set for hearing on *oral argument* before the appellate court. Sometimes the court itself will ask for argument; otherwise, one of the parties may petition for it. Often, appeals are submitted *on the briefs* without argument.

Courts of appeal do not hear further evidence, and it is unusual for any of the parties to the case to attend the hearing of the oral argument.

Generally, the case has been assigned to one of the judges of the appellate court, although the full court will hear the argument. Thereafter, it is customary for all the judges to confer on the issues presented, and then the judge who has been assigned the case will write an opinion. If a judge or judges disagree with the result, they may dissent and file a *dissenting opinion*. In many states, a written opinion is required.

An appellate court will usually not weigh evidence and generally will reverse a trial court for errors of law only.

Not every error of law will warrant a reversal. Some are *harmless errors* — that is, the rights of a party to a fair trial were not prejudiced by them.

However, an error of law, such as the admission of improper and persuasive evidence on a material issue, may and often does constitute a *prejudicial* and *reversible error.*

After the opinion is *handed down* and time for the filing of a petition for rehearing—or a petition for transfer, or a petition for *writ of certiorari* (if there is a higher appellate court)—has expired, the appellate court will send its *mandate* to the trial court for further action in the case.

If the lower court is *affirmed*, the case is ended; if reversed, the appellate court may direct that a new trial be held, or that the judgment of the trial court be modified and corrected as prescribed in the opinion.

The taking of an appeal ordinarily does not suspend the operation of a judgment obtained in a civil action in a trial court. Thus, the party prevailing in the trial court may order an execution issued on the judgment, unless the party appealing filed an *appeal* or *supersedeas bond*, which binds the party and his surety to pay or perform the judgment in the event it is affirmed on appeal. The filing of this bond will *stay* further action on the judgment until the appeal has been concluded.

CHAPTER NINETEEN

The Rules of the Game

Statutes and rules governing expert witnesses vary from court to court. There are state rules and Federal rules; there are rules of evidence and rules of civil procedure. Some of the more important Federal rules are reproduced here for ready reference. The name and location of the rules for each state are listed.

Ask your client-attorney which court is trying the case; which rules will apply. You will also want to obtain copies of the rules for each state you work in. Visit the *law* library, (probably) in the courthouse of your nearest large town or county seat. If the county seat is too far away, try a university law school.

A list of the statutes and rules governing expert witnesses in Federal Court as well as for each state follows.

The Federal Rules of Evidence are contained in Rules 702, 703, 704, 705, 706, and 803 (3), (4), and (18).

Rule 702. If scientific, technical, or other specialized knowledge will assist the trier of fact to understand the evidence or to determine a fact in issue, a witness qualified as an expert by knowledge, skill, experience, training, or education, may testify thereto in the form of an opinion or otherwise.

Rule 703. The facts or data in the particular case upon which an expert bases an opinion or inference may be those perceived by or made known to him at or before the hearing. If of a type reasonably relied upon by experts in the particular field in forming opinions or inferences upon the subject, the facts or data need not be admissible in evidence.

Rule 704. Testimony in the form of an opinion or inference otherwise admissible is not objectionable because it embraces an ultimate issue to be decided by the trier of fact.

Rule 705. The expert may testify in terms of opinion or inference and give his reasons therefore without prior disclosure of the underlying facts or data, unless the court requires otherwise. The expert may in any event be required to disclose the underlying facts or data on cross-examination.

Rule 706.

(a) Appointment. The court may on its own motion or on the motion of any party enter an order to show cause why expert witnesses should not be appointed, and may request the parties to submit nominations. The court may appoint any expert witnesses agreed upon by the parties, and may appoint expert witnesses of its own selection. An expert witness shall not be appointed by the court unless he consents to act. A witness so appointed shall be informed of his duties by the court in writing, a copy of which shall be filed with the clerk, or at a conference in which the parties shall have opportunity to participate. A witness so appointed shall advise the parties of his findings, if any; his deposition may be taken by any party; and he may be called to testify by the court or any party. He shall be subject to cross-examination by each party, including a party calling him as a witness.

(b) Compensation. Expert witnesses so appointed are entitled to reasonable compensation in whatever sum the court may allow. The compensation thus fixed is payable from funds which may be provided by law in criminal cases and civil actions and proceedings involving just compensation under the Fifth Amendment. In other civil actions and proceedings the compensation shall be paid by the parties in such proportion and at such time as the court directs, and thereafter charged in like manner as other costs.

(c) Disclosure of appointment. In the exercise of its discretion, the court may authorize disclosure to the jury of the fact that the court appointed the expert witness.

(d) Parties' experts of own selection. Nothing in this rule limits the parties in calling expert witnesses of their own selection.

Rule 803.

(3) Then existing mental, emotional, or physical condition. A statement of the declarant's then existing state of mind, emotion, sensation, or physical condition (such as intent, plan, motive, design, mental feeling, pain, and bodily health), but not including a statement of memory or belief to prove the fact remembered or believed unless it relates to the execution, revocation, identification, or terms of declarant's will.

(4) Statements for purposes of medical diagnosis or treatment. Statements made for purposes of medical diagnosis or treatment and describing medical history, or past or present symptoms, pain, or sensations, or the inception or general character of the cause or external source thereof insofar as reasonably pertinent to diagnosis or treatment.

(18) Learned treatises. To the extent called to the attention of an expert witness upon cross-examination or relied upon by him in direct examination, statements contained in published treatises, periodicals, or pamphlets on a subject of history, medicine, or other science or art, established as a reliable authority by the testimony or admission of the witness or by other expert testimony or by judicial notice. If admitted, the statements may be read into evidence but may not be received as exhibits.

Federal Rules of Civil Procedure:
See Rules 26, 30, 35, and 45.

State statutes and rules governing expert witnesses.
(RCP = Rules of Civil Procedure, RE = Rules of Evidence)

Alabama
RCP - Rules 16 and 26
Sec. 12-21-40
Sec. 12-21-160
Sec. 12-21-181

Alaska
Rules of Court Procedure and Administration - Rules 16 and 26.

Arizona
RCP - Rules 16 and 26
Rules of Criminal Procedure - Rules 15.1 and 15.2
Rules of Evidence 701-706
Sec. 12-348
Sec. 12-567
Sec. 13-1621
Sec. 13-1673
Sec. 41-191.02
Sec. 45-545

Arkansas
RCP - Rules 16 and 26
RE - Rules 701-706

California
Business & Professions Code - Sec. 6726
Code of Civil Procedure - Sec. 998, Sec. 1031.5, Sec. 1768, Sec. 2016, Secs. 2037-2037.9
Evidence Code - Secs. 703-703.5, Secs. 720-723, Secs. 730-733, Secs. 771-773, Secs. 800-805, Secs. 810-822, Sec. 870, Secs. 893-897, Sec. 1418.
Penal Code - Sec. 1027, Sec. 1107, Sec. 1127b
Welfare & Institution Code - Secs. 6307-6311

Colorado
RCP - Rules 16 and 26

Connecticut
Sec. 45-78u
Sec. 45-78y
Sec. 52-149a
Sec. 52-260
Sec. 53a-204

Delaware
Common Pleas, Court Civil Rules - Rules 16 and 26
RE - Rules 701-706

District of Columbia
RCP - Rules 16 and 26
Sec. 14-308

Florida
RCP - Rule 1.390
Secs. 90.701-90.706

Indiana
Rules of Trial Procedure - Rules 16 and 26
Sec. 34-1-14-12

Iowa
RCP - Rule 122
Sec. 86.8
Sec. 622.25
Sec. 622.72
Sec. 691.2
Sec. 749A.2
Sec. 813.2, Rule 10

Sec. 813.2, Rule 19
Sec. 815.4
Sec. 815.5

Kansas
Sec. 60-216
Sec. 60-226
Secs. 60-456 et seq.

Kentucky
RCP - Rules 16 and 26
Rules of Criminal Procedure - Rule 9.46
Ch. 406.091
Ch. 406.101

Georgia
Sec. 38-1710
Sec. 81A-116
Sec. 81A-126

Hawaii
RE - Rules 701-706
Sec. 571-46
Sec. 704-410

Idaho
Sec. 7-1117
Sec. 7-1118
Sec. 18-4110
Sec. 19-4303
Sec. 37-2507
Sec. 37-2508

Illinois
Ch. 38, P.113-3
Ch. 38, P.115-6
Ch. 42, P.4024
Ch. 110, P.58
Ch. 110A, P.218

Louisiana
Code of Civil Procedure - 192 and 1424
Code of Criminal Procedure - 660

Sec. 9:396 et seq.
Sec. 13:1601
Sec. 13.3666
Secs. 15:464 et seq.
Secs. 39:1481 et seq.
Sec. 40:639

Maine
Title 19 Sec. 279

Maryland
Rules of Procedure - Rules 400 and 536
Courts and Judicial Proceedings, Sec. 9-120
Art. 27, Sec. 13

Massachusetts
RCP - Rules 16 and 26
Ch. 156 Sec. 95
Ch. 231 Sec. 60E
Ch. 233 Sec. 79C

Michigan
District Court Rules - Rule 605
General Court Rules - Rules 302.4, 302.7,
302.8, 605

Minnesota
RCP for District Courts - Rules 26.05, 16, 16.02
RE - Rules 701-708
Sec. 257.69
Sec. 357.25
Sec. 563.01

Mississippi
Sec. 11-1-6
Sec. 13-1-226
Sec. 41-37-21
Sec. 61-1-31
Sec. 71-3-57
Sec. 93-9-21
Sec. 93-9-23
Sec. 93-9-25
Sec. 93-9-27
Sec. 99-21-13(3)

Missouri
Supreme Court Rules - Rule 25.09

Montana
RCP - Rules 16 and 26
RE - Rules 701-706
Sec. 26-2-505
Sec. 46-11-312
Sec. 46-4-203
Sec. 46-14-213

Nebraska
Sec. 3-118
Sec. 19-706
Secs. 25-12, 115 et seq.
Sec. 25-1220
Secs. 27-702-27-706
Sec. 28-815
Secs. 49-14, 104

Nevada
RCP - Rules 16,26, and 53
Sec. 17.115
Secs. 18.005 et seq.
Sec. 37.190
Sec. 50.045
Sec. 50.275
Sec. 50.285
Sec. 50.305
Secs. 50.315 et seq.
Sec. 52.045
Sec. 56.020
Sec. 172.135
Sec. 175.271
Sec. 205.170
Sec. 533.175

New Hampshire
Sec. 281:39

New Jersey
Rules Governing Civil Practice - Rule 4:10-2
Sec. 2A:83-2
Sec. 2A:83-3

Sec. 2A:84A, Rule 19

New Mexico
RCP - Rules 16 and 26
RE - Rules 701-706
Sec. 38-6-4

New York
Banking Law, Sec. 6022(8g)
Civil Practice Law & Rules - Sec. 3036, Sec. 3101,
Sec. 3114, Sec. 4515
Criminal Procedure Law, Sec. 190.30(2)
Education Law, Sec. 6510(7)
Eminent Domain Procedure Law, Sec. 508, Sec. 602,
Sec. 701
General Obligations Law, Sec. 5-1502H(8)
Public Officers Law,Sec. 17(1)
Rapid Transit Law, Sec. 60(b)

North Carolina
Sec. 1-A-1, Rules 16 and 26
Sec. 7A-314(d)
Sec. 7A-454
Secs. 8-58.12-8-58.14

North Dakota
RCP - Rule 16 and 26
RE - Rules 701-708
Rule of Criminal Procedure - Rule 28
Sec. 11-19-09
Sec. 28-26-06
Sec. 29-26-13

Ohio
RCP - Rules 16 and 26
RE - Rules 701-706
Sec. 117.03
Sec. 120.04
Sec. 307.52
Sec. 2743.43

Oklahoma
Title 10 Secs. 501 et seq.
Title 12 Sec. 433
Title 12 Sec. 2604

Title 12 Sec. 2615
Title 12 Sec. 2701-12, Sec. 2706
Title 12 Sec. 2803
Title 12 Sec. 3009
Title 21 Sec. 1040.18
Title 21 Sec. 1083
Title 22 Sec. 701
Title 59 Sec. 585
Title 66 Sec. 55
Title 76 Sec. 21

Oregon
Sec. 20.098
Sec. 40.410
Sec. 40.415
Sec. 40.420
Sec. 40.425
Sec. 42.280
Sec. 109.254
Sec. 109.256
Sec. 109.260

Pennsylvania
RCP - Rules 4003.5
Title 26 Sec. 1-701-26, Sec. 1-705
Title 52 Sec. 30.63
Title 53 Sec. 11011

Rhode Island
Superior Court & District Court Rules of Civil Procedure -
Rules 16 and 26
Superior Court & District Court Rules of Criminal
Procedure - Rule 28
Sec. 9-17-19
Sec. 9-17-20
Sec. 9-17-22
Sec. 9-19-30

South Carolina
Rules of Practice for the Circuit Courts of South
Carolina - Rule 90
Sec. 16-3-26
Sec. 16-15-280
Sec. 19-5-410

Sec. 19-19-210

South Dakota
Sec. 15-6-16
Sec. 15-6-26
Secs. 19-15-2-19-15-19

Tennessee
RCP - Rules 16, 26.02, 26.05
Sec. 24-7-114

Texas
RCP - Rule 166
Code of Criminal Procedures - Rules 26.05 & 26.05-5
Art. 3737b

Utah
RCP - Rules 16 and 26
RE - Rules 56-58
Sec. 58-37a-4
Sec. 77-35-15
Secs. 78-25-18-78-25-23
Secs. 78-45a-7-78-45a-10

Vermont
RCP - Rules 16 and 26
Title 12 Sec. 1643

Virginia
Medical Malpractice Rules of Practice - Rule 7
Sec. 8.01-401.1
Sec. 8.01-581.20
Sec. 14.1-190
Sec. 19.2-168
Sec. 19.2-168.1

Washington
RCP - Rules 16 and 26
RE - Rules 701-706
Sec. 10.77.100
Sec. 15.52.020
Sec. 15.53.200
Sec. 26.12.170

West Virginia
RCP - Rules 16 and 26
Rules of Criminal Procedure - Rule 28

Wisconsin
Sec. 32.06
Sec. 32.17
Sec. 59.14
Sec. 256.65
Sec. 269.55
Sec. 269.65
Sec. 271.04
Sec. 448.02
Sec. 757.65
Sec. 767.47
Sec. 802.11
Sec. 804.011
Sec. 804.07
Sec. 806.05
Sec. 879.41
Sec. 885.235
Sec. 906.02
Secs. 907.01-907.07
Sec. 973.06
Sec. 975.06
Sec. 979.06

Wyoming
RCP - Rules 16 and 26
RE - Rules 701-706
Sec. 1-14-102
Sec. 1-14-104

APPENDIX

Glossary of Terms

The following definitions of terms are of interest to the expert witness. For further information see the many texts on the subject. *Black's Law Dictionary* provides definitions for thousands of legal terms.

Acquittal: The verdict in a criminal trial in which the defendant is found not guilty.

Action: The formal legal demand of one's rights from another person brought in court. A lawsuit.

Adjudication: The formal pronouncing or recording of a judgment or decree by a court. The court's final order.

Adversary System: The system of trial practice in the U.S. and some other countries in which each of the opposing, or adversary, parties has full opportunity to present and establish its opposing contentions before the court.

Affidavit: A written statement or declaration of facts sworn to by the maker, taken before a person officially permitted by law to administer oaths.

Allegation: The assertion, declaration, or statement of a party to a action, made in a pleading, setting out what he or she expects to prove.

Amicus Curiae: Literally, friend of the court. A party with strong interest in, or views on, the subject matter of the dispute will petition the court for permission to file a brief, ostensibly on behalf of a party but actually to suggest a rationale consistent with its own views.

Answer: The pleading filed by the defendant in response to plaintiff's complaint.

Appearance: The formal proceeding by which a defendant submits himself to the jurisdiction of the court.

Appellant: The party appealing a decision or judgment to a higher court.

Appellee: The party against whom an appeal is taken (usually, but not always, the winner in the lower court). It should be noted that a party's status as appellant or appellee bears no relation to his status as plaintiff or defendant in the lower court.

Arbitration: The hearing and settlement of a dispute between opposing parties by a third party who is not a judge. This decision is often binding by prior agreement of the parties.

Arraignment: In criminal practice, to bring a prisoner to the bar of the court to answer to a criminal charge.

Bailiff: A court attendant whose duties are to keep order in the courtroom and to have custody of the jury.

Best Evidence: Primary evidence; the best evidence which is available; any evidence falling short of this standard is secondary; i.e., an original letter is best evidence compared to a copy.

Bifurcation: The splitting of a case into separate issues.

Brief: (1) In American law practice, a written statement prepared by the counsel arguing a case in court. It contains a summary of the facts of the case, the pertinent laws, and an argument of how the law applies to the facts supporting counsel's position; or (2) A summary of a published opinion of a case prepared for studying the opinion in law school.

Burden of Proof: In the law of evidence, the necessity or duty of affirmatively proving a fact or facts in dispute.

Calendar: Can mean the order in which cases are to be heard during a term of court. The *Martindale-Hubbel Law Directory* contains calendars for state and federal courts, and includes the name of the court, the name of the judge, and the date of the term's beginning.

Case in Point: A judicial opinion which deals with a factual situation similar to the one being researched and substantiates a point of law to be asserted. (Also called a *Case on All Fours*.)

Case Law: The law of reported appellate judicial opinions as distinguished from statutes or administrative law.

Cause of Action: A claim in law and in fact sufficient to bring the case to court; the grounds of an action. (Example: breach of contract.)

Cause: A suit, litigation or action—civil or criminal.

Chambers: Private office or room of a judge.

Change of venue: The removal of a suit begun in one county or district, to another, for trial, or from one court to another in the same county or district.

Chattel: Any article of personal property, as opposed to real property. It may refer to animate as well as inanimate property.

Circuit Courts: Originally, courts whose jurisdiction extended over several counties or districts, and whose sessions were held in such counties or districts alternately; today, a circuit court may hold all its sessions in one county.

Circumstantial Evidence: All evidence of indirect nature; the process of decision by which court or jury may reason, from circumstances known or proved to establish by inference, the principal fact.

Citation: The reference to authority (previous cases) necessary to substantiate the validity of one's argument or position.

Civil Law: (1) Roman law embodied in the Code of Justinian which presently prevails in most countries of Western Europe other than Great Britain and which is the foundation of Louisiana law (civil law verses common law); (2) the law concerning non-criminal matters in a common law jurisdiction (civil law verses criminal law).

Claim: (1) The assertion of a right, as to money or property; (2) the accumulation of facts which give rise to a right enforceable in court.

Class Action: A lawsuit brought by a representative party on behalf of a large group, all of whose members have the same or a similar grievance against the defendant. Used when the group is too large for it to be practical to name every member of the group as a party.

Code: By popular usage a compilation or a revised statute. Technically, the laws in force are rewritten and arranged in classified order, with the addition of material having the force of law taken from judicial decrees. The repealed and temporary acts are eliminated and the revision is re-enacted.

Codification: The process of collecting and arranging systematically, usually by subject, the laws of a state or country. The end product may be called a code, revised code or revised statutes.

Commit: To send a person to prison, an asylum, workhouse, or reformatory by lawful authority.

Common Law: The origin of the Anglo–American legal systems. English common law was largely customary law and unwritten, until discovered, applied, and reported by the courts of law. In theory, the common law courts did not create law but rather discovered it in the customs and habits of the English people. The strength of the judicial system in pre-parliamentary days is one reason for the continued emphasis in common law systems on case law (prior decisions). In a narrow sense, common law is the phrase still used to distinguish case law from statutory law.

Complaint: The plaintiff's initial pleading which is no longer full of the technicalities demanded by the common law. A complaint need only contain a short and plain statement of the claim upon which relief is sought, an indication of the type of relief requested, and an indication that the court has jurisdiction to hear the case.

Condemnation: The legal process by which real estate of a private owner is taken for public use without his consent, but upon the award and payment of just compensation.

Consideration: Something to be done or abstained from, by one party to a contract, in order to induce another party to enter into a contract. Usually refers to money.

Contempt of Court: Any act calculated to embarrass, hinder, or obstruct a court in the administration of justice, or calculated to lessen its authority or dignity. Contempts are of two kinds: direct and indirect. Direct contempts are those committed in the immediate presence of the court; indirect is the term chiefly used with reference to the failure or refusal to obey a lawful order.

Conversion: The wrongful appropriation to oneself of the personal property of another.

Conveyance: The transfer of title to property from one person to another.

Corpus Delicti: The body (material substance) upon which a crime has been committed; e.g., the corpse of a murdered person, the charred remains of a burned house.

Corroborating Evidence: Evidence supplementary to that already given and tending to strengthen or confirm it.

Costs: An allowance for expenses in prosecuting or defending a suit. Ordinarily does not include attorney's fees.

Count: A separate and independent claim. A civil petition or a criminal indictment may contain several counts.

Counterclaim: A claim presented by a defendant in opposition to the claim of a plaintiff; it constitutes a separate cause of action.

Cross-examination: The questioning of a witness in a trial, or in the taking of a deposition, by the party opposed to the one who produced the witness.

Damages: Monetary compensation awarded by a court for an injury caused by the act of another. Damages may be *actual* or *compensatory* (equal to the amount of loss shown), *exemplary* or *punitive* (in excess of the actual loss and which is given to punish the person for the malicious conduct which caused the injury), or *nominal* (less than the actual loss-- often a trivial amount such as one dollar) which is given because the injury is slight or because the exact amount of injury has not been determined satisfactorily.

Decree: A decision or order of the court. A final decree is one which fully and finally disposes of the litigation; an interlocutory decree is a provisional or preliminary decree which is not final.

Default: A default in an action of law occurs when a defendant omits to plead within the time allowed or fails to appear at the trial.

Defendant: The person against whom a civil or criminal action is brought.

Demur: To file a pleading (called a *demurrer*) admitting the truth of the facts in the complaint, or answer, but contending they are legally insufficient.

Deposition: A form of oral testimony taken by the opposing attorney in advance of the trial with a court reporter present to record every word. See Chapter Ten.

Direct Evidence: Proof of facts by witnesses who saw acts done or heard words spoken, as distinguished from circumstantial evidence, which is called indirect.

Direct Examination: The first interrogation of a witness by the party on whose behalf he is called.

Directed Verdict: An instruction by the judge to the jury to return a specific verdict.

Dismissal Without Prejudice: Permits the complainant to sue again on the same cause of action, while dismissal *with prejudice* bars the right to bring or maintain an action on the same claim or cause.

Docket Number: A number, sequentially assigned by the clerk at the outset to a lawsuit brought to a court for adjudication.

Double Jeopardy: Common-law and constitutional prohibition against more than one prosecution for the same crime, transaction or omission.

Due Care: The legal duty one owes to another according to the circumstances of a particular case.

Due Process: Law in its regular course of administration through the courts of justice. The guarantee of due process requires that every person have the protection of a fair trial.

Felony: A crime of a graver nature than a misdemeanor. Generally, an offense punishable by death or imprisonment in a penitentiary.

Fraud: An intentional perversion of truth; deceitful practice or device resorted to with intent to deprive another of property or other right, or in some manner to do him injury.

Garnishment: A proceeding whereby property, money or credits of a debtor, in possession of another (the garnishee), are applied to the debts of the debtor.

Grand Jury: A jury of inquiry whose duty is to receive complaints and accusations in criminal cases, hear the evidence and find bills of indictment in cases where they are satisfied that there is probable cause that a crime was committed and that a trial ought to be held.

Habeas Corpus: *You have the body.* The name given a variety of writs whose object is to bring a person before a court or judge. In most common usage, it is directed to the official or person detaining another, commanding him to produce the body of the prisoner or person detained so the court may determine if such person has been denied his liberty without due process of law.

Hearings: Extensively employed by both legislative and administrative agencies and can be adjudicative or merely investigatory. Adjudicative hearings can be appealed in a court of law. Congressional committees often hold hearings prior to enactment of legislation; these hearings are then important sources of legislative history. Adjudicative hearings are like trials.

Hearsay: Evidence not proceeding from the personal knowledge of the witness, such as a rumor.

Hornbook: The popular reference to a series of textbooks which review a certain field of law in summary, textual form, as opposed to a casebook which is designed as a teaching tool and includes many reprints of court opinions.

Hostile Witness: A witness who is subject to cross–examination by the party who called him to testify, because of his evident antagonism toward that party as exhibited in his direct examination.

Hypothetical Question: A combination of facts and circumstances, assumed or proved, stated in such a form as to constitute a coherent state of facts upon which the opinion of an expert can be asked by way of evidence in a trial.

Impeachment of Witness: An attack on the credibility of a witness by the testimony of other witnesses.

In Camera: In the judge's chambers; in private.

Inadmissible: That which, under the established rules of evidence, cannot be admitted or received.

Indictment: An accusation in writing found and presented by a grand jury, charging that a person therein named has done some act, or been guilty of some omission, which, by law, is a crime.

Injunction: A judge's order that a person do or, more commonly, refrain from doing a certain act. An injunction may be preliminary or temporary pending trial of the issue presented, or it may be final if the issue has already been decided in court.

Instruction: A direction given by the judge to the jury concerning the law of the case.

Interlocutory: Provisional; temporary; not final. Refers to orders and decrees of a court.

Interrogatories: A series of formal written questions sent to the opposing side. The opposition must provide written answers under oath. Typically the asking side is fishing for information and the answering side is as vague as legally possible.

Intervention: A proceeding in a suit or action by which a third person is permitted by the court to make himself a party.

Irrelevant: Evidence not relating or applicable to the matter in issue; not supporting the issue.

Jurisdiction: The power given to a court by a Constitution or a legislative body to make legally binding decisions over certain persons or property.

Jurisprudence: (1) The science or philosophy of law; (2) a collective term for case law, as opposed to legislation.

Jury: A certain number of persons, selected according to law, and sworn to inquire of certain matters of fact, and declare the truth upon evidence laid before them.

Key Number: Part of the major indexing system devised for American case law, developed by West Publishing Company. The key number is a permanent number given to a specific point of this case law.

Leading Question: One which instructs a witness how to answer or puts into his mouth words to be echoed back; one which suggests to the witness the answer desired. Prohibited on direct examination.

Liability: The condition of being responsible either for damages resulting from an injurious act or for discharging an obligation or debt.

Libel: A method of defamation expressed by print, writing, pictures, or signs. In its most general sense, any publication that is injurious to the reputation of another.

Lien: A claim against property as security for a debt, under which the property may be seized and sold to satisfy the debt.

Limitation: A certain time allowed by statute in which litigation must be brought. Statute of limitations.

Litigate: To bring a civil action in court.

Local Counsel: A local attorney who assists an out-of-town attorney in the litigation of a case.

Malfeasance: Evil doing; ill conduct; the commission of some act which is positively prohibited by law.

Mandamus: The name of a writ which issues from a court of superior jurisdiction, directed to an inferior court, commanding the performance of a particular act.

Mandate: A judicial command or precept proceeding from a court or judicial officer, directing the proper officer to enforce a judgment, sentence, or decree.

Material Evidence: Such as is relevant and goes to the substantial issues in dispute.

Misdemeanor: Offenses less than felonies; generally those punishable by fine or imprisonment otherwise than in penitentiaries.

Misfeasance: A misdeed or trespass; the improper performance of some act which a person may lawfully do.

Mistrial: An erroneous, abortive or invalid trial; a trial which cannot stand in law because of lack of jurisdiction, wrong drawing of jurors, or disregard of some other fundamental requisite.

Mitigating Circumstance: One which does not constitute a justification or excuse for an offense, but which may be considered as reducing the degree of moral culpability.

Moot: Unsettled; undecided. A moot point is one not settled by judicial decisions.

Motion: A formal request made to a judge pertaining to any issue arising during the pendency of a lawsuit.

Negligence: The failure to do something which a reasonable man, guided by ordinary considerations, would do; or the doing of something which a reasonable and prudent man would not do.

Nexus: A connection between groups or series.

Nolo Contendere: A pleading usually used by defendants in criminal cases, which literally means *I will not contest it.*

Nonfeasance: Failure to act. Failure to do what ought to be done.

Objection: The act of taking exception to some statement or procedure in trial. Used to call the court's attention to improper evidence or procedure.

Of Counsel: A phrase commonly applied to counsel employed to assist in the preparation or management of the case, or its presentation on appeal, but who is not the principal attorney of record.

Out of Court: One who has no legal status in court is said to be *out of court*; i.e., he is not before the court. For example, when a plaintiff, by some act of omission or commission, shows that he is unable to maintain his action, he is frequently said to have put himself *out of court*.

Panel: A list of jurors to serve in a particular court, or for the trial of a particular action; denotes either the whole body of persons summoned as jurors for a particular term of court or those selected by the clerk by lot.

Parties: The persons who are actively concerned in the prosecution or defense of a legal proceeding.

Percipient Witness: One who was there and saw what happened.

Peremptory Challenge: The challenge which the prosecution or defense may use to reject a certain number of prospective jurors without giving any explanation or reason.

Petit Jury: The ordinary jury of twelve (or fewer) persons for the trial of a civil or criminal case. So called to distinguish it from the grand jury.

Petition: A formal, written application to a court requesting judicial action on a certain matter.

Petitioner: The person presenting a petition to a court, officer, or legislative body; the one who starts an equity proceeding or the one who takes an appeal from a judgment.

Plaintiff: A person who brings an action; the party who complains or sues in a personal action and is so named on the record.

Plea Bargaining: The process whereby the accused and the prosecutor in a criminal case work out a mutually satisfactory disposition of the case. It usually involves the defendant's pleading guilty to a lesser offense or to only one or some of the counts of a multi-count indictment in return for a lighter sentence than that possible for the graver charge.

Pleading: The process by which the parties in a suit or action alternately present written statements of their contentions, each responsive to that which precedes, and each serving to narrow the field of controversy, until there evolves a single point, affirmed on one side and denied on the other, called the *issue* upon which they then go to trial.

Polling the Jury: A practice whereby the jurors are asked individually whether they assented, and still assent, to the verdict.

Power of Attorney: An instrument authorizing another to act as one's agent or attorney.

Prejudicial Error: Synonymous with *reversible error*; an error which warrants the appellate court to reverse the judgment before it. Distinguished from *harmless error*, which does not merit reversal.

Preliminary Hearing: Synonymous with *preliminary examination*; the hearing given a person charged with a crime by a magistrate or judge to determine whether he or she should be held for trial. Since the Constitution states that a person cannot be accused in secret, a preliminary hearing is open to the public unless the defendant requests that it be closed. The accused person must be present at this hearing and must be accompanied by his or her attorney.

Preponderance of evidence: In a civil case, the plaintiff must prove their case and the defendant must prove any defenses asserted by a preponderance of evidence. This is the greater weight of the credible evidence which may be less than the proof beyond reasonable doubt, which would be required in a criminal case.

Presumption of Fact: An inference as to the truth or falsity of any proposition of fact, drawn by a process of reasoning in the absence of actual certainty of its truth or falsity, or until such certainty can be ascertained.

Presumption of Law: A rule of law that courts and judges shall draw a particular inference from a particular fact, or from particular evidence.

Procedural Law: That law which governs the operation of the legal system, including court rules and rules of procedure, as distinguished from substantive law.

Prosecutor: One who instigates the prosecution upon which an accused is arrested, or one who brings an accusation against the party whom he suspects to be guilty; also, one who takes charge of a case and performs the function of trial lawyer for the people.

Quash: To overthrow; vacate; to annul or void a summons or indictment.

Reasonable Doubt: In a criminal case, an accused person is entitled to acquittal if, in the minds of the jury, his guilt has not been proved beyond a *reasonable doubt*; that state of the mind of the jurors in which they cannot say they feel an abiding conviction as to the truth of the charge.

Rebuttal: The introduction of rebutting evidence; the showing that statements of witnesses as to what occurred are not true; the stage of a trial at which such evidence may be introduced.

Redirect Examination: Follows cross–examination and is exercised by the party who first examined the witness.

Referee: A person to whom a cause pending in a court is referred by the court to take testimony, hear the parties, and report thereon to the court. He is an officer exercising judicial powers and is an arm of the court for a specific purpose.

Remand: To send back for further proceedings, as when a higher court sends back to a lower court.

Resolution: A formal expression of the opinion of a rule-making body adopted by the vote of that body.

Respondent: The party who makes an answer to a bill in an equity proceeding or who contends against an appeal.

Rest: A party is said to *rest* or *rest his case* when he has presented all the evidence he intends to offer.

Retainer: Act of the client in employing his attorney or counsel; and also denotes the fee which the client pays when he retains the attorney to act for him.

Rules of Court: Rules that regulate practice and procedure before the various courts. In most jurisdictions, these rules are issued by the court itself, or by the highest court in that jurisdiction.

Slander: Base and defamatory spoken words tending to harm another's reputation, business or means of livelihood. Both *libel* and *slander* are forms of defamation—the former expressed by print, writings, pictures or signs; the latter orally.

Stare Decisis: The doctrine of English and American law which states that when a court has formulated a principle of law as applicable to a given set of facts, it will follow that principle and apply it in future cases where the facts are substantially the same. It connotes the decision of present cases on the basis of past precedent.

State's Evidence: Testimony given by an accomplice or participant in a crime, tending to convict others.

Statute: The written law in contradistinction to the unwritten law.

Statutes of Limitations: Laws setting time periods during which disputes may be taken to court.

Stay: A stopping or arresting of a judicial proceeding by order of the court.

Stipulation: An agreement by attorneys on opposite sides of a case as to any matter pertaining to the proceedings or trial.

Subpoena: A process to order a witness to appear and give testimony before a court or magistrate.

Subpoena Duces Tecum: A process by which the court commands a witness to appear and produce certain documents, records, or other physical things in a trial.

Substantive Law: That law which establishes rights and obligations as distinguished from procedural law, which is concerned with rules for establishing their judicial enforcement.

Summons: A writ directing the sheriff or other officer to notify the named person that an action has been commenced against him in court and that he is required to appear, on the day named, and answer the complaint in such action.

Testimony: Oral evidence given by a competent witness, under oath, as distinguished from evidence derived from writings and other sources.

Tort: An injury or wrong committed, either with or without force, to the person or property of another.

Transcript: The official record of proceedings in a trial or hearing.

Trespass: An unlawful interference with one's person, property, or rights. At common law, trespass was a form of action brought to recover damages for any injury to one's person or property or relationship with another.

Trier of Fact: The jury in a *jury trial*. The judge in a (no jury) *court trial.*

Venire: Technically, a writ summoning persons to court to act as jurors; popularly used as meaning the body of names thus summoned.

Venue: The particular county, city or geographical area in which a court with jurisdiction may hear and determine a case.

Verdict: In practice, the formal and unanimous decision or finding made by a jury, reported to the court and accepted by it.

Waiver of Immunity: A means authorized by statutes by which a witness, in advance of giving testimony or producing evidence, may renounce the fundamental right guaranteed by the Constitution that no person shall be compelled to be a witness against himself.

Warrant of Arrest: A writ issued by a magistrate, justice, or other competent authority, to a sheriff, or other officer, requiring him to arrest a person therein named and bring him or her before the magistrate or court to answer to a specified charge.

Weight of Evidence: The balance or preponderance of evidence; the inclination of the greater amount of credible evidence, offered in a trial, to support one side of the issue rather than the other.

Willful: A willful act is one done intentionally, without justifiable cause, as distinguished from an act done carelessly or inadvertently.

With Prejudice: The term, as applied to judgment of dismissal, is as conclusive of rights of parties as if action had been prosecuted to final adjudication adverse to the plaintiff.

Without Prejudice: A dismissal *without prejudice* allows a new suit to be brought on the same cause of action.

Witness: One who testifies to what he or she has seen, heard, or otherwise observed.

Writ: An order issuing from a court of justice and requiring the performance of a specified act, or giving authority and commission to have it done.

Directories and Registries

Write to each directory and registry for information on their services and an application. Some directories offer free listings and some charge. Most registries charge a percentage of your fee for each case referred to you. See Chapter Two. For more registries, usually in more specific disciplines, see *Lawyer's Desk Reference*.

Forensic Services Directory
National Forensic Center
Betty Lipscher
17 Temple Terrace, Suite 401
Lawrenceville, NJ 08648
(800) 526-5177, (609) 883-0550

Lawyers Desk Reference
Harry M. Philo, Esquire (Editorial)
18490 Wildemere, Suite 442
Detroit, MI 48221
(313) 862-6285

Expert Witness Index Service
Marylou Calzaretta
Defense Research Institute
750 North Lake Shore Drive #500–A
Chicago, IL 60611
(312) 944-0575

Technical Advisory Service for Attorneys (TASA)
428 Pennsylvania Avenue, Suite 770
Fort Washington, PA 19034
(215) 643-5252

Technical Advisory Service for Attorneys (TASA)
608 East Missouri Avenue
Phoenix, AZ 85012
(602) 248-8464

Aerospace Consultants Directory
Automotive Consultants Directory
Society of Automotive Engineers
400 Commonwealth Drive, #620
Warrendale, PA 15096-0001
(412) 776-4970

Expert Witness Network
Gary Melickian
George S. Jenkins
1608 New Hampshire Avenue NW #G-100
Washington, DC 20009-2512
(202) 667-6961
(800) 345-5993

Technical Assistance Bureau (medical only)
Joseph Gentile
11484 Washington Plaza West # 108-A
Reston, VA 22090
(800) 336-0190

Register of Experts (for the construction industry)
American Bar Association
750 North Lake Shore Drive, 10th Floor
Chicago, IL 60611
(312) 988-5000

Consultants and Consulting Organizations Directory
Editorial Services Limited (Editorial)
Janice W. McLean
P.O. Box 6789-B
Silver Spring, MD 20906
(301) 871-5280

Professional Organizations and Important Addresses

Here is a list of general forensic and other related organizations. For specific consulting organizations, see the *Encyclopedia of Associations* and *National Trade and Professional Associations*. Ask for them at the reference desk of your public library. You may wish to join some of these organizations and/or contact them about buying membership directories or renting membership mailing lists for promotional mailings.

National Forensic Center
Betty Lipscher
17 Temple Terrace, Suite 401
Lawrenceville, NJ 08648
(800) 526-5177 (609) 883-0550

American Academy of Forensic Sciences
Beth Ann Lipskin, Ex Dir.
225 South Academy Blvd #A-201
Colorado Springs, CO 80910
(303) 596-6006

Canadian Society of Forensic Science
JoAnne Cottingham
2660 Southvale Crescent #215-C
Ottawa, ON   K1B 4W5
Canada
(613) 731-2096

American Standards Testing Bureau
John L. Zimmerman
40 Water Street
New York, NY 10004
(212) 943-3156

American Standards Testing Bureau
2525 Hyperion Avenue
Los Angeles, CA 90027
(213) 661-6900, (213) 666-6900

American Society for Testing and Materials
116 Race Street
Philadelphia, PA 19103
(215) 299-5400

American National Standards Institute
1430 Broadway
New York, NY 10018
(212) 354-3300

American Society of Mechanical Engineers
345 East 47th Street
New York, NY 10017
(212) 705-7051

Underwriters Laboratories (UL)
Publications Stock
333 Pfingsten Road
Northbrook, IL 60062
(312) 272-8800

National Safety Council
444 North Michigan Avenue
Chicago, IL 60611
(312) 527-4800

Int'l Society of Air Safety Investigators
Washington National Airport
West Building #259
Washington, DC 20001
(202) 521-5195

American Association of Professional Consultants
912 Union Street
Manchester, NH 03104
(603) 623-5378

American Bar Association
750 North Lake Shore Drive, 10th Floor
Chicago, IL 60611
(312) 988-5000

Assn of Trial Lawyers of America
1050 31st Street NW
Washington, DC 20007
(202) 965-3500

Lawyer-Pilots Bar Association
John S. Yodice, Esquire
600 Maryland Avenue SW #701
Washington, DC 20024
(202) 863-1000

NTSB Bar Association
P.O. Box 65461
Washington, DC 20036-5461

Books

Books of interest to the expert witness are listed below. For a more complete (though less specific) list, including books aimed at certain area specialties, see the *Forensic Bibliography* published by the National Forensic Center. Some of the most useful and important books to the expert witness are reviewed in detail near the end of this book and are available from Para Publishing. See the order blank on the last page.

Forensic Bibliography
National Forensic Center
17 Temple Terrace, Suite 401
Lawrenceville, NJ 08648
(800) 526-5177 (609) 883-0550

Guide to Experts' Fees
National Forensic Center
17 Temple Terrace, Suite 401
Lawrenceville, NJ 08648
(800) 526-5177 (609) 883-0550

Expert Witness Handbook,
Tips and Techniques for the Litigation Consultant
Dan Poynter
(See the order blank)

Expert Witness Checklists
Douglas Danner
Lawyers Co-operative Publishing Co.
Aqueduct Building, #660
Rochester, NY 14694
(716) 546-5530
-and-
Bancroft-Whitney Company
301 Brannan Street, #421
San Francisco, CA 94107
(415) 986-4410

Lawyers' Desk Reference
Technical Sources for Conducting a Personal Injury Action
Harry M. Philo, Esquire
Lawyers Co-operative Publishing Company (editorial)
Aqueduct Building, #660
Rochester, NY 14694
(716) 546-5530
-and-
Bancroft-Whitney Company
301 Brannan Street, #421
San Francisco, CA 94107
(415) 986-4410

California Expert Witness Guide
Raoul D. Kennedy
Continuing Education of the Bar
2300 Shattuck Avenue, Suite 142
Berkeley, CA 94704
(415) 642-6810 (213) 825-5301

Preparing Witnesses for Trial (Course material)
California Continuing Education of the Bar
2300 Shattuck Avenue, Suite 142
Berkeley,CA 94704
(415) 642-6810 (213) 825-5301

What Makes Juries Listen
Sonya Hamlin
Prentice-Hall, Law & Business
855-D Valley Road
Clifton, NJ 07013
(201) 472-7400

Jury Trials, The Psychology of Winning Strategy
Donald E. Vinson
The Mitchie Company
P.O. Box 7587-B
Charlottesville, VA 22906-7587
(800) 446-3410

The Expert Witness in Litigation
Hirsch and Pemberton
Defense Research Institute
750 North Lake Shore Drive
Chicago, IL 60611
(312) 944-0575

The Expert Witness
Peter Dorram
Planners Press
American Planners Association
1313 East 60th Street
Chicago, IL 60637
(312) 955-9100

Using Experts in Civil Cases
Melvin D. Kraft
Practicing Law Institute
810 Seventh Avenue
New York, NY 10019
(212) 765-5700

Depositions, Expert Witnesses and Demonstrative Evidence in Personal Injury Cases (course handout)
David G. Miller
Practicing Law Institute
810 Seventh Avenue
New York, NY 10019
(212) 765-5700

Forensic Accounting: The Accountant as Expert Witness
Francis C. Dykeman
Wiley Interscience
605 Third Avenue
New York, NY 10158
(800) 225-5945

Marketing Your Consulting and Professional Services
Richard A Connor, Jr. & Jeffrey P. Davidson
Wiley Interscience
605 Third Avenue
New York, NY 10158
(800) 225-5945

The Use of Economists in Antitrust Litigation
American Bar Association Press
750 North Lake Shore Drive
Chicago, IL 60611
(312) 988-6062

The Role of Experts in Business Litigation
American Bar Association Press
750 North Lake Shore Drive
Chicago, IL 60611
(312) 988-6062

Expert Witness Handbook: A Guide for Engineers
D.G. Sunar, Ph.D.
Professional Publications
P.O. Box 199-A
San Carlos, CA 94070
(415) 593-9119

Thinking on Your Feet
Marian K. Woodall
(See the order blank)

Air Crash Investigation of General Aviation Aircraft
Glenn Ellis
Capstan Publications, Inc.
P.O. Box 306-E
Basin, WY 82410
(307) 568-2604

How to Become a Successful Consultant in Your Own Field
Hubert Bermont
The Consultant's Library
P.O. Box 309-B
Glenelg, MD 21737
(301) 531-3560

The Consultant's Kit
Jeffrey L. Lant, Ph.D.
(See the order blank)

Also contact the American Bar Association and Prentice-Hall Law & Business for videotapes on expert witness subjects.

Periodicals

Send for sample copies of, and subscription information on, the following periodicals. Some magazines and newsletters accept expert witness advertising. For more listings, check the periodical directories available at the reference desk of your public library.

The Expert and the Law
National Forensic Center
17 Temple Terrace, Suite 401
Lawrenceville, NJ 08648
(800) 526-5177, (609) 883-0550

Trial Magazine
Assn of Trial Lawyers of America
1050 31st Street NW
Washington, DC 20007
(202) 965-3500

ABA Journal
American Bar Association
750 North Lake Shore Drive
Chicago, IL 60611
(312) 988-5000

California Lawyer
State Bar of California
555 Franklin Street
San Francisco, CA 94102
(415) 561-8280

The Advocate
Los Angeles Trial Lawyers Association
2140 West Olympic Blvd
Los Angeles, CA 90015
(213) 487-1212

CTLA Forum
California Trial Lawyers Association
1020 12th Street, 3rd Floor
Sacramento, CA 95814

Lawyer-Pilots Bar Association Journal
1100 Huntington Building
Cleveland, OH 44115
(216) 696-1100

Consultants News
Kennedy and Kennedy, Inc
Templeton Road
Fitzwilliam, NH 03447
(603) 585-6544

Consulting Opportunities Journal
J. Stephen Lanning
5000 Kaetzel Road
Gapland, MD 21736
(301) 432-4242

Conferences and Courses

Write for descriptions, schedules and prices.

National Forensic Center
Betty Lipscher
17 Temple Terrace, Suite 401
Lawrenceville, NJ 08648
(800) 526-5177, (609) 883-0550

University of Southern California
Inst. of Safety and Systems Management
Los Angeles, CA 90089-0021
(213) 743-6523

California Continuing Education of the Bar
Preparing Witnesses for Trial
2300 Shattuck Avenue
Berkeley, CA 94704
(415) 642-0223

International Association of Forensic Sciences
(Held every three years)
801-750 Jervis Street
Vancouver, BC   V6E 2A9
Canada
(604) 681-5226

Index

Also see the Glossary

The Expert Witness Bookshelf

The following books may be ordered from Para Publishing. See the order blank. Your satisfaction is guaranteed on all books. Order any book, look it over and feel free to return it if not completely satisfied.

WRITING

Is There a Book Inside You?, How to Successfully Author a Book Alone or Through Collaboration by Dan Poynter and Mindy Bingham. As an expert witness, your book will validate your expertise and lend credibility to what you say. Now you can *author* a book whether or not you have the time or ability to be a good *writer*. This book reveals how to find, interview, negotiate, contract and work with writing partners such as editors, researchers, contract writers, co-authors, and ghostwriters. *Is There a Book Inside You?* will show you how to pick your topic, how to break the project down into easy-to-attack pieces, how and where to do research, a way to improve your material with a step-by-step process that makes writing (almost) easy, and more. Writer's Digest Book Club main selection

ISBN 0-915516-42-X Softcover
5.5 x 8.5 240 pages $9.95

Writing with Precision by Jefferson D. Bates. A practical and systematic approach to writing clearly and precisely. A good resource with numerous examples and fun to read. Should be read by every author before writing a manuscript and every publisher before editing a book.

ISBN 0-87491-185-0 Softcover
6 x 9 226 pages $7.95

Write Right! by Jan Venolia. This desk drawer digest of punctuation, grammar and style is an important reference which should be next to your dictionary. Demonstrating proper usage with quotes from literature and politics, *Write Right!* makes editing reports and books easy and fun. This style manual is essential when copy editing.

ISBN 0-89815-061-2 Softcover
5.5 x 7 127 pages $4.95

GETTING ORGANIZED - MOTIVATION

A Whack on the Side of the Head by Roger von Oech. The author describes the ten mental locks that prevent you from being more innovative — and explains how to open them. You will learn the difference between hard and soft thinking, why breaking the rules leads to innovation, how impractical ideas lead to practical creative ideas, why play is the father of invention, why the third right answer is usually more creative, why a *whack on the side of the head* can be the best thing to happen to you, and much more. Fascinating, useful and fun; one of our top sellers.

ISBN 0-911121-00-5 Softcover
7.5 x 10.5 141 pages $9.95

A Kick in the Seat of the Pants, Using Your Explorer, Artist, Judge and Warrior to be More Creative by Roger von Oech. If you liked *Whack on the Side of the Head*, you will love the sequel. The human body has two ends on it: one to create and one to sit on. Sometimes people get their ends reversed — and they need a kick in seat of the pants. Von Oech provides exercises, stories, tips and proven techniques to straighten out each of your creative roles. Get your thinking going. Inspiring.

ISBN 0-06-096024-8 Softcover
7.5 x 10.5 153 pages $8.95

PUBLISHING

The Self-Publishing Manual, How to Write, Print & Sell Your Own Book is a complete course in writing, publishing, marketing, promoting and distributing books. It takes the reader step–by–step from idea, through manuscript, printing, promotion and sales. Along with an in-depth study of the book publishing industry, the book explains in detail numerous innovative book marketing techniques. *The Manual* is a *Bible* for writers and a constant reference for publishers. It is must reading for expert witnesses.

ISBN 0-915516-37-3 Softcover
5.5 x 8.5   352 pages $14.95

Publishing Short–Run Books, How-to Paste up and Reproduce Books Instantly Using Your Quick Print Shop is a revolutionary concept in short–run book manufacture. This is the ideal system for expert witnesses who want a book to validate their expertise, educators needing just a few copies for a class, business managers needing a special look for a presentation, authors who are trying to get the attention of a publisher (it is easier to sell a book than a manuscript), poets who desire a small private printing, and anyone who is in a hurry to break into print.

ISBN 0-915516-23-3 Softcover
5.5 x 8.5   100 pages $5.95

How to Get Happily Published by Judith Appelbaum and Nancy Evans. How to write, find a publisher, locate an agent or publish yourself by two women with years of varied experience in New York publishing. Learn how book publishing works. This is a gold mine of publishing information with a lengthy resource section.

ISBN 0-452-25332-2 Softcover
5.25 x 8   271 pages $6.95

The Writer's Survival Manual by Carol Meyer explains how to get your book published. The author shows how to find the right publisher or agent, discusses the contract and provides ideas on marketing as well as details on subsidiary rights. Contains an example of an author-publisher contract. Good reference.

ISBN 0-517-54485-7 Softcover
4.25 x 7   316 pages $4.95

PROMOTION

How to Get Publicity and Make the Most of it Once You've Got it by William Parkhurst. Get your name in the papers, your voice on the radio, your face on TV. How to book and conduct radio, television and print interviews. Parkhurst covers writing news releases, designing press kits and more. Good, solid and practical with an insider's expertise. Like having your own publicist on your bookshelf. No one wants to be surprised in an interview situation. Excellent reference.

ISBN 0-8129-1161-X Hardcover
6 x 8.5 245 pages $14.95

The Unabashed Self-Promoter's Guide by Jeffrey Lant, Ph.D. Lant is a master at obtaining free publicity and then pyramiding it to promote more publicity. In this book, he shows how to generate articles about yourself and your book, how to arrange and handle print and radio/TV interviews, while providing promotional ideas, samples and contracts.

ISBN 0-940374-06-4 Softcover
8.5 x 11 366 pages $29.95

CONSULTING

The Consultant's Kit by Jeffrey Lant, Ph.D. Turn your expertise into extra income. Lant tells how to define your specialty, establish a network, market your experience, contracting, setting up shop and running your consulting business. Valuable information for expert witnesses.

ISBN 0-940374-07-2 Softcover
8.5 x 11 205 pages $29.95

Tricks of the Trade, the Complete Guide to Succeeding in the Advice Business by Jeffrey Lant, Ph.D. This is a sequel to *The Consultant's Kit*, expanded, updated and with new information.

ISBN 0-940374-10-2 Softcover
8.5 x 11 316 Pages $29.95

SPEAKING

How to be an Outstanding Speaker by John L. Dutton reveals the eight secrets of speaking success. Expert witnesses must be able to get their point across effectively. Dutton shows how to understand your audience, design your speech, he provides presentation tips, covers researching, discusses advance questions and more.

ISBN 0-9615335-5-2 Softcover
5.5 x 8.5 232 pages $13.95

Speaking for Money by Gordon Burgett and Mike Frank is about **seminars** and speaking. Burgett provides inside information gained from years in the seminar business. Frank tells you how to turn your subject into (lecturing) cash. If you like to talk about your subject, this book will show you how to profit while you spread the word.

ISBN 0-910167-00-1 Softcover
6 x 9 224 pages $9.95

Thinking on Your Feet by Marian K. Woodall will help you to answer the questions well, whether you know the answers or not. Woodall studies tough questions and tells you how to turn them in to easier questions. Interesting techniques. Get this book — don't get caught without an answer.

ISBN 0-941159-01-9 Softcover
5.5 x 8.25 100 pages $9.95

Order Form

Para Publishing
Post Office Box 4232-P
Santa Barbara, CA 93140-4232 USA
Telephone (805) 968-7277

I am enclosing $_____ Please send the following books. I understand that I may return any books for a full refund – for any reason, no questions asked.

( ) Expert Witness Handbook @ $29.95
( ) Consultant's Kit @ $29.95
( ) How to be an Outstanding Speaker @ $13.95
( ) How to Get Happily Published @ $6.95
( ) How to Get Publicity @ $14.95
( ) Is There a Book Inside You? @ $9.95
( ) Kick in the Seat of the Pants @ $8.95
( ) Publishing Short-Run Books @ $5.95
( ) Speaking for Money @ $9.95
( ) The Self-Publishing Manual @ $14.95
( ) Thinking on your Feet @ $9.95
( ) Tricks of the Trade @ $29.95
( ) Unabashed Self-Promoter's Guide @ $29.95
( ) Whack on the Side of the Head @ $9.95
( ) Write Right! @ $4.95
( ) Writer's Survival Manual @ $4.95
( ) Writing with Precision @ $7.95

Name:_____

Address:_____

City:_____State:____ Zip:_____

Please add **sales tax** of 6% for books shipped to California addresses.
Shipping
Book Rate: $1.50 for the first book and 75 cents for each additional book. (Surface shipping may take three to four weeks)
Air Mail: $3 per book.
( ) Please add my name to the Expert Witness Grapevine so that I may receive more information
Call in an order using your Visa or Master Card

Order Form

Satisfaction Guaranteed

Para Publishing
Post Office Box 4232-P
Santa Barbara, CA 93140-4232 USA
Telephone (805) 968-7277

I am enclosing $_____ Please send the following books. I understand that I may return any books for a full refund—for any reason, no questions asked.

( ) Expert Witness Handbook @ $29.95
( ) Consultant's Kit @ $29.95
( ) How to be an Outstanding Speaker @ $13.95
( ) How to Get Happily Published @ $6.95
( ) How to Get Publicity @ $14.95
( ) Is There a Book Inside You? @ $9.95
( ) Kick in the Seat of the Pants @ $8.95
( ) Publishing Short-Run Books @ $5.95
( ) Speaking for Money @ $9.95
( ) The Self-Publishing Manual @ $14.95
( ) Thinking on your Feet @ $9.95
( ) Tricks of the Trade @ $29.95
( ) Unabashed Self-Promoter's Guide @ $29.95
( ) Whack on the Side of the Head @ $9.95
( ) Write Right! @ $4.95
( ) Writer's Survival Manual @ $4.95
( ) Writing with Precision @ $7.95

Name:_____

Address:_____

City:_____State:____ Zip:_____

Please add **sales tax** of 6% for books shipped to California addresses.
Shipping
Book Rate: $1.50 for the first book and 75 cents for each additional book. (Surface shipping may take three to four weeks)
Air Mail: $3 per book.
( )   Please add my name to the Expert Witness Grapevine so that I may receive more information
Call in an order using your Visa or Master Card